Why do so many governments both subsidize water use and then pay people not to use it? Zetland's message is powerful and convincing. If you are concerned about water scarcity, pay attention to the economics of water use.

Mike Young, Gough Whitlam and Malcolm Fraser Chair
in Australian Studies, Harvard University
Chair in Water and Environmental Policy, University of Adelaide
Honorary Professor, University College London

This field guide to water management includes real-world examples to illustrate the challenges and opportunities available to those who fully engage with the many sides of scarcity. If you want to understand the real importance of taking the same measured approach to water that we do with other scarce resources, this is your book.

Paul W. Lander, PhD, ASLA, LEED AP
Lecturer, Geography & Sustainable Practices Program
University of Colorado-Boulder

Water policy commonly lacks common sense. In this book, using basic economics, David Zetland successfully inserts some badly needed sense into the discussion. It should be required reading for anyone who wants to avoid future shortages of water.

Fredrik Segerfeldt, Author
Water for Sale

David Zetland draws on common sense economics to illustrate how policies that reflect water scarcity to end users can help address many of the water quality and quantity challenges of the 21st century. Concise yet insightful, *Living with Water Scarcity* offers an empowering program for each of us to seek positive change at our locus in the water system.

Joshua Abbott, Associate Professor
Environmental & Resource Economics, School of Sustainability
Arizona State University

David Zetland embraces the reality of water scarcity but describes a wise and prudent political economy to ensure adequate water for all our human and environmental needs. Water managers and, most importantly, their political leaders, will benefit from this articulate and accessible roadmap to a more sustainable regime of water management.

G. Tracy Mehan, III, former Assist;
US Envirc

People think of water as something sacred and valuable that "should" be free. So we sprinkle it as if it were holy, but we also use clean, fully potable water to transport raw sewage from our home miles away to a treatment plant. David Zetland tries to bring a bit of rationality to this mass of contradictions by explaining why we can't go on this way. Our real choice is simple: pay more for something sensible, or pay less for nothing. Zetland's humor makes the book fun to read; his serious point makes it imperative to read.

Michael Munger, Professor
Departments of Economics and Political Science, Duke University

An economic perspective on water topics that embraces the reality of too little water to satisfy the 21st century thirsts of cities, farms, and the environment, and lays out common sense economic approaches that may shape a better future. My favorite quote from Zetland's very readable text: "We must be patient with water managers, regulators and politicians who learned their trades in an age of abundance."

David Carle, Author
Introduction to Water in California, Traveling the 38th Parallel: A Water Line around the World, and *Water and the California Dream*

In concise writing Dr. Zetland offers economic solutions for water problems in a world where overpopulation and mismanagement have done great damage to nature and the environment. Economy, just like modern technology, owes ecology an apology. If read critically, this book could bring a sea change in an economic climate where scarcity is abundant and money often flows like water — down the drain.

Michael van der Valk, Hydrologist and Scientific Secretary
Netherlands National Committee IHP-HWRP (UNESCO & WMO)

Living with Water Scarcity is an elegant little book that applies common sense economics and calm rhetoric to a hot-button issue. Its message is that scarcity is inevitable, so we should learn to live with it. We can use the same tools to manage scarcity as we do with other basic goods. It goes beyond a mechanical application of textbook economics by bringing in political and environmental perspectives. Read, enjoy, learn.

Ed Dolan, Author
There Ain't No Such Thing as a Free Lunch — A Libertarian Perspective on Environmental Policy

Whether you agree with him or not, Dr. Zetland continues to advance the thinking on economic frameworks for addressing the world's water problems. I happen to agree with him a lot.

Richard Rauschmeier, California Water Policy Advisor

This short book gives a lucid and humane account of many of the key policy issues concerning the water sector that the world must face. Its proposals are economically literate and practical. Anyone interested in how these problems can be tackled in rich and poor countries will benefit from reading it.

Martin Cave, Professor
Imperial College Business School

With the Colorado River's Lake Mead again shrinking towards crisis levels, record droughts and floods becoming the new normal, and chronic groundwater depletions striking even historically wet regions like the Mississippi Delta and the southeastern U.S., *Living with Water Scarcity* is an essential survival manual for comprehending and managing our predicament. Zetland's book should be read by every water manager, city councilman, and concerned water citizen.

Steven Solomon, Author
WATER: The Epic Struggle for Wealth, Power, & Civilization

Are water shortages inevitable during severe droughts? Read this book to learn the deceptively simple answer: no. Zetland delivers a clear and concise account of water scarcity and potential solutions for it. *Living with Water Scarcity* is engaging and accessible to a broad and diverse audience. It will equip readers with the basic building blocks to solve complex water challenges today and in the future. I recommend it highly.

Dustin Garrick, Philomathia Chair of Water Policy
McMaster University

Living with Water Scarcity brings out the author's message — with which I mostly agree — clearly, effectively, and forcefully. Water may seem a simple issue — just make sure that it is provided to all who need it. But water issues are complex and multidimensional. The book has successfully touched on most of them in a way that is accessible to readers who are willing to go carefully over its presentation and arguments. Water People should be thankful.

Yoav Kislev, Professor Emeritus
Agricultural Economics and Management, The Hebrew
University of Jerusalem

Canadians and others are profligate overusers of water and habitual under-investors in its protection. That is at least partly because apprehension about potential commodification of water has made many citizens unreceptive to any discussion of water in economic terms. But as shortages of useable water in a changing climate become the norm, we will have no choice but to explore ways to better harness market forces to the goal of sustainability. In a remarkably accessible style, David Zetland explores a myriad of ways that can be approached. David's book, *Living with Water Scarcity*, along with his popular Aguanomics blog will no doubt move the yardsticks forward on this critically important public dialogue.

Ralph Pentland, Author
Down the Drain

Elinor Ostrom showed us how in the real world ordinary people can (and do) reverse the hypothetical "tragedy of the commons" by self-organizing around shared natural resources like wells, streams and wetlands. That Nobel laureate has passed into history, but her spirit is alive and well in the clear words, critical mind, and pragmatic outlook of another California water obsessive, David Zetland.

James G. Workman, Author
Heart of Dryness and co-founder of SmartMarkets

With *Living with Water Scarcity*, Zetland returns with even simpler messages than those conveyed in his celebrated *End of Abundance*. Shorter, wittier, and more persuasive, I read *Living with Scarcity* from cover to cover in one shot, mesmerized by his clear thinking and sharp focus on helping us learn to live with water scarcity.

Alberto Garrido, Associate Professor
Agricultural Economics, Polytechnic University of Madrid
Deputy Director of the Water Observatory

Water scarcity is perhaps a more pressing issue than global warming. Here is an excellent book which informs quickly on how to manage water for society as a whole rather than unfettered private individuals and firms.

Rick van der Ploeg, Professor
Economics, University of Oxford
Research Director, Oxford Centre for the Analysis of Resource
Rich Economies (OxCarre)

Living with Water Scarcity

David Zetland

Aguanomics Press

Amsterdam ~ Mission Viejo ~ Vancouver

2014

Cover design by Nic Newton (www.nicnewton.com). Illustrations by Allison Choppick (www.allisonchoppick.carbonmade.com). Cover photo by David Zetland. Author photo by Hugh Zetland.

Typeset in Baskervald ADF with LATEX on April 1, 2014.

ATTN: Quantity discounts available for 20+ copies. Please contact the author at dzetland@gmail.com.

Version 1.0. Visit www.livingwithwaterscarcity.com for updates.

Publisher's Cataloging in Publication
Zetland, David

Living with water scarcity / David Zetland — 1st ed.
p.   cm.
Summary: "Don't panic. It is easy to live with water scarcity. Use politics to allocate community water before using economics to ration commodity water." — Provided by publisher.
Includes index.

ISBN-13: 978-0615932187   LCCN: 2013916596

1. Water resources development — Economic aspects 2. Water resources development — Government policy I. Title
HD1691.Z48 2014

Contents

The rise of scarcity   1
Water for the community before water for the economy

I   **Water for me *or* you**
Prices and markets reconcile different values for water

1   **Water as a commodity**   9
Manage water according to its use

2   **Water on tap**   17
Subsidies increase waste and reduce reliability

3   **Water for profit**   33
Properly regulated businesses add value

4   **Recycled water**   41
Dirty water must be cleaned — and can be sold

5   **Food and water**   51
Water markets help farmers produce more with less

II   **Water for *us***
Transparency and engagement improve social outcomes

6   **Water for the community**   67
Citizens must hold their leaders to account

7   **A human right to water**   77
Poor people need money and choices more than rights

8   **Pipes, canals and dams**   85
Infrastructure endures, so be careful who pays

9   **Water wars**   95
Solve conflict locally to help citizens

10   **Environmental flows**   101
Healthy environments keep us alive and happy

From afterword to forward   109
A few words of thanks   111
Index   115

The rise of scarcity

Scarcity is a perception. Shortage is a fact. Most of us deal with scarcity every day. We spend our time going places, doing things and seeing people. We spend our money on products and services. We wouldn't mind a bit more time and money, but at least we get some of what we want.

Shortage is worse than scarcity because you can't get any of what you want, even if you have time or money.

Increasing water scarcity is forcing us to choose among competing wants. Some lucky people do not face these choices, but an increasing number do. Those people need to manage scarcity if they want to avoid shortage.

This book is not about measuring scarcity, a perception that changes from one place to another and one community to another. This book describes appropriate solutions for living with — perhaps even thriving with — water scarcities in both quantity and quality.

Why aren't these solutions being used now? The good news is that they are being used in some places, and I'll tell you about them. The bad news is that they are not being used in many other places. I can think of four barriers to these solutions. First, water managers trust systems that have worked for centuries. They do not experience the pain of scarcity and do not want to work now for benefits later. Second, the current system benefits special interests that block change. Third, water customers have a hard time communicating their frustrations to complex water monopolies that may be slow to answer the phone. Finally, politicians and regulators may be too biased to see the need for change or too busy to promote it.

Keep those barriers in mind as we learn how to live with
scarcity and prevent shortage. We can overcome them with
a destination, a map and hope. This book should give you a
little more of each.

The end of abundance

Scarcity is like the fuel warning light in your car. Ignore it for
too long, and you'll be stranded. People who grew up with
water abundance may not see the flashing light. Their atti-
tudes and habits — and the social, economic and political
institutions that reinforce them — make it hard to respond
to water scarcity. Neighbors who share water from rivers,
lakes, or aquifers may refuse to acknowledge that there is
not enough water for every need. Others fight to get their
"fair" share. A third group wants to address scarcity, but
they cannot without help from others.

We see these perspectives when discussing environmental water flows. Some people want them because they feel
ecosystems are beautiful and useful. Others would rather divert water to direct economic uses. Both sides are right, but
they need to compromise.

Compromise is built on common foundations, and all of
us have a stone to contribute. We cannot just worry about
environmental flows. We must also consider water quality,
service to the poor, groundwater reserves, irrigation systems,
safety from floods, and other water-related facets of life. All
these issues share a common root in water scarcity, which
gets worse with an increase in demand, a fall in supply, or
both.

Water demand rises with population and wealth. Additional people will take additional showers, but wealthy people will use more water in their power showers.

The supply of water on the planet is fixed, but useful
supplies are not. We have reduced supply by depleting underground aquifers, polluting fresh water and leaking water
from dilapidated infrastructure. The water will come back
eventually, but we may not be able to wait so long.

It is not always clear whether a rise in demand or drop

in supply is responsible for scarcity. A drought that reduces flows into a city's reservoir certainly decreases supply, but can we blame water scarcity on the drought — or the fact that the city is in the middle of a desert?

We can overcome scarcity by erecting dams, building desalination plants or drilling deeper wells, but those supply-side solutions are costly. Dams block rivers. Desalination plants are energy-intensive. Deeper wells borrow water from our neighbors and the future. Most important, additional supply is worthless if it is soon overcome by rising demand.

Water demand has been allowed to grow for centuries because the benefits of using water are so great. The greatest advances in human longevity arrived when we figured out how to bring clean water to our homes and take dirty water away. We found many other ways to enjoy water's blessings and encouraged people to enjoy those blessings by giving water away, for free. Now water is scarce.

We can reduce our demands for water, but we need to do so with the understanding that water flows through our lives in complex ways. We cannot rely on prices and markets alone to ration demand. We must also consider and integrate the cultural, social and environmental values that water supports in our lives and communities. These reasons should clarify why we need to manage commodity water with economic tools and community water with political mechanisms. I will spend more time on commodity and community

water in the next chapter. For now, just assume that commodity uses do not affect others and community water must
be managed as a shared resource.

The political economy of water

Housewives practiced the earliest "home economics" of getting as many meals as possible from a limited budget of time,
money and other resources. We use the same economics outside the home. We choose food from a menu according to
our taste and budget. When we travel, we trade between
fast and cheap. We wear clothes that balance among style,
comfort and activity. Academics call these decision processes "microeconomic" because they belong to individuals.
"Macroeconomic" outcomes such as unemployment rates or
trade flows reflect the interaction and aggregation of individual microeconomic decisions, but we will ignore them in
this book because water management does not usually affect
bank interest rates. The economics we want to discuss describe the microeconomic choices of people like you and me.
We will call those choices "economic" to save space.

Economics is useful for understanding water management in an era of scarcity because economists — like housewives — want to get as many benefits as possible from scarce
resources. We do this by looking at how policies create incentives that lead to decisions, and whether the outcomes
resulting from those decisions match the original goals of
the policies. We want to know, in other words, if the road
we are following ends up at our chosen destination.

Although most people associate economics with prices
and markets, economists also spend a lot of time thinking
about how people interact outside of markets. Policies, incentives and decisions in home, office, and social settings
often reflect non-price decisions and group dynamics. Most
people do not associate economics with these dynamics; they
talk about "the politics" of the situation. I will follow that
everyday use here while noting that politics and economics
have always interacted. Contemporary economics descends
from the much older study of "moral philosophy and politi-

cal economy." This book reflects that tradition by integrating ideas from economics, politics, and moral justice.

Unraveling the tangle of flows

Interacting economics and politics complicate water management. I have tried to simplify matters by grouping chapters into two parts. Part I covers economic topics in which one person's action or water use does not *necessarily* affect others. A bottled water company need not affect agricultural irrigation; long showers do not prevent green lawns. Part II covers political topics in which people's decisions or uses interact. A dam changes flood risks, environmental flows, and the cost of irrigation. The separation of personal topics in Part I from social topics in Part II clarifies whether we should rely primarily on economic or political tools. It also helps us divide complex problems into simpler economic and political parts that can be addressed separately or sequentially.

The first chapter in each part discusses its theme: economics in Part I and politics in Part II. Subsequent chapters focus on particular private or social topics. The table of contents lists chapters and their main themes.

Chapters in Part I can also be paired with their related partners in Part II. Chapters 1 and 6 develop complementary ideas on economics and politics. Chapter 2 discusses drinking water as a commodity service. Chapter 7 looks at whether a right to drinking water makes that service likely. These parallels continue with chapter pairs of 3/8, 4/9 and 5/10. There is no need to read chapters in pairs, but it sometimes helps to see how a "simple" economic use in Part I can turn into a complex political issue in Part II.

The book's ordering of parts and chapters does not imply that water should be managed in that order. Indeed, it is often necessary to resolve political issues before implementing economic policies. It is not possible, for example, to set the right price for drinking water (Chapter 2) without an engaged and knowledgeable regulator (Chapter 6). Allocations to farmers (Chapter 5) should, for similar reasons, only occur after water is set aside for the environment (Chapter 10).

Water flows through our lives in many ways. Sometimes water arrives on its own. Sometimes we bring it to us. These interactions mean that water management must respond to fluctuating water cycles *and* changing human priorities. The good news is that efficient management helps in all conditions. The tools we use to allocate scarce water during droughts can allocate scarce land during floods. We clean water to drink, but we also clean wastewater to discharge.

I hope this book clarifies how scarcity emerges, who bears its costs, and how to prevent shortages. I have tried to be reasonable, but I expect you to read critically. Examples may reflect unique conditions. Solutions may not be compatible with your local traditions. My main goal is to get you to think differently about problems, causes and responses. Then you can decide how to address water issues that matter to you.

Note: I have kept this book as simple and short as possible. Visit www.livingwithwaterscarcity.com for references, case studies and resources.

Part I

Water for me *or* you

CHAPTER 1

Water as a commodity

Water is a simple molecule, but we possess it in complex ways. The water in a glass is yours, but we all own the water in a river. These complications can paralyze water management discussions in which people emphasize different dimensions of water flows. The classification of water into a personal or social possession clarifies how we should manage it.

Four goods possessed two ways

How does one decide whether a use is personal — leaving someone free to use the water as they like, without fear of affecting other people — or social, meaning that one person's use affects others?

Economists classify a good as one of four types — private, club, common pool, or public — depending on whether it is *rival* or not and *excludable* or not. We can show those characteristics in a table:

	excludable	non-excludable
rival	private goods	common-pool goods
non-rival	club goods	public goods

Water is rival if two people cannot use it twice or simultaneously. You and I cannot both drink the same (rival) water, but we can swim in the same (non-rival) river.

Water is excludable if others can be legally kept from using it. I can exclude you from my water glass, but I cannot keep you from jumping into a river from your boat. Excludable water is the same as commodity water that can be — and should be — owned and managed as a personal possession. Someone holding "their" water is best able to protect, enjoy and value it. Non-excludable water can be enjoyed — or spoiled — by anyone. That water, like the flow of a river, needs to be managed by the community that shares it. Community management makes it possible for many to enjoy shared water without damaging it.

The characteristics of rival/non-rival and excludable/non-excludable clarifies the type of good and how it should be managed, but management must adapt when changing circumstances transform a good from one type to another.

Water in a swimming pool, for example, is a non-rival and non-excludable public good for a few swimmers, but it will turn into a rival, non-excludable common pool good if too many swimmers show up. Over-crowding reduces benefits for everyone, so it makes sense to update access policies. Rivalry can be reduced by dividing the pool into lap-swimming and play areas or setting separate times for swimming and play. Those rules will turn the pool into a non-rival, excludable club good that everyone can enjoy at the right place or time.

The key point — and my main point — is that we should manage water as the good it *is*, not the good it *was*. Old rules from a past of abundance are inappropriate in scarcity, so we need a new management paradigm in which we identify what type of good water is, decide what type of good it should be, and change institutions to move towards our goals. This plan will require that we read Part I for excludable personal uses (private and club goods) and Part II for non-excludable social uses (common pool and public goods).

Rival private and common pool goods appear in both parts because rivalry can be managed through economic *or* political means. A swimming pool can be run by a private club with rules or by a municipal operator that sets prices to limit access. The correct management technique will depend on local institutions. Reforms won't work if they ignore past practices and cultural norms.

Scarcity and shortage, demand and supply

Scarcity and shortage are the same for water as they are for other goods — except that most goods are traded in markets in which rising and falling prices balance supply and demand to prevent shortages.

Consider gasoline. People demand it for their cars and gas stations supply it, but those everyday facts obscure the complexity of a supply chain that brings oil from halfway around the world to billion-dollar refineries that feed a distribution system that always seems to have enough gas for you and me. The supply chain for water is shorter and simpler, but it is more likely to experience shortages.

Why? Regulators require that monopoly water suppliers charge a price that covers the cost of delivery. This cost does not include a scarcity price for water because most monopolies pay nothing for their water. That administrative cost of zero is far below the value of water to consumers or the cost of shortage, but regulators do not allow utilities to charge more. This pro-consumer regulation will leave consumers thirsty unless it is updated to reflect the interaction of demand and supply.

Price determines how much we buy of what we like

Economists study demand in two dimensions. A "demand schedule" reflects our taste for a good at a range of prices. Taste depends on culture, income, the prices of other goods, and so on. Coffee drinkers like coffee at all prices. Coffee haters are not even interested in free coffee.

Our "quantity demanded" depends on price. We basically look at the price, think about our demand schedule, and then choose how much we want. Coffee drinkers may order an extra cup if coffee is cheap because they have "elastic" demand that responds to price changes.

There are three key ideas here. First, changes in tastes

or income weaken or strengthen our demand. I will drink more coffee if I get a raise. Second, price affects the *quantity* demanded, given these tastes. I will drink less coffee if its price rises. Finally, it is much easier to reduce quantity demanded by increasing prices than it is to reduce demand by changing someone's taste. Don't tell me coffee is bad if you want me to drink less. Raise its price.

The two dimensions of demand also apply to water. Our taste for water depends on how we use it. We have a very inelastic demand for the daily 4–5 liters of water we need to live, which means we will pay anything to get it. Our taste is weaker for the *additional* water we use for lawns, showers and so on. Our demand for those uses is elastic. Elasticity explains why people have green lawns where water is cheap and take shorter showers when water is expensive.

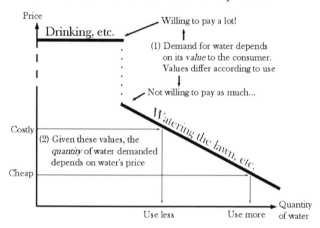

This figure illustrates those differences. (Academics must forgive me for emphasizing willingness to pay over elasticity.) It shows how we are willing to pay a lot for drinking water and less for other uses. With cheap prices, we get our drinking water and "more" water for other uses. If price rises, we will still consume drinking water (its value is far greater than the price we have to pay), but we use less water in other ways, because those uses are "not worth it."

Can we charge for water scarcity when we need water to live? The answer is "perhaps" when it comes to poor people in developing countries (Chapter 7) but "yes" when it comes to people in developed countries. It makes no sense to subsidize water prices to people who can easily afford the full cost of water.

Scarcity pricing will not result in thirst and death. Prices help people prioritize their water uses. Some will stop watering their lawns; others may take shorter showers so they can water their gardens. On an industrial scale, higher prices increase water recycling at factories, efficient irrigation on farms, and so on.

It is easy to predict that higher prices will reduce total water use, but it is hard to predict how higher prices will affect individuals. Some people will make big changes in their water consumption; others hardly any. The focus should not be on individual actions as much as their collective impact.

Supply reflects costs, sometimes

The supply of a good depends on production technology. Technology combines raw materials, machines, labor and knowledge into a good that has a cost. An improvement in technology will lower costs, thereby increasing the supply available at any given price. Old fashioned cobblers, for example, used time and skills to turn leather, rubber, nails, and thread into shoes that were relatively expensive. They have been replaced with low-skilled people using specialized machines to make standardized shoes from artificial materials on the other side of the world. Technology dictates the cost of supplying different quantities of a good, but prices determine actual quantity supplied. A higher price increases quantity supplied because producers are paid enough to cover the extra cost of pushing their technology.

Water supply works the same way. The cost of supply depends on water's origin, quality, distance, and so on. Cost falls when pumps get more efficient, but it rises when raw water is dirtier. Taking technology as given, higher prices can pay for deeper pumping, worker overtime, and other means of increasing supply. Can we supply our way out of scarcity? We can spend money on new supply, but that supply will be overwhelmed by additional demand if consumers do not pay the full cost of delivering their water.

That caveat may seem obvious, but many water utilities collect $1.50 for water that costs $2 to deliver. They may set prices to cover historical costs of $1.50 or set prices based on the average cost of different sources. They almost always omit the scarcity value of water. These practices are not fiscally prudent, but they are widespread. Historical costs may be used because the utility is not setting aside funds for capital renovations. Average costs are used because the utility does not want to collect excess revenues and "make profits."

As an example, consider a utility that gets half its water from a source that costs $1 per unit and the other half from a source that costs $2 per unit. The utility may try to charge $1 for half its water and $2 for the other half, but customers will complain if they do not get enough cheap water (the next chapter covers block rate pricing). A price of $2 per unit generates "profits" and more complaints. A compromise solution sells all units for $1.50. No business would ever sell $2 water for $1.50, but a monopolistic utility can because its price is usually so cheap that it can sell all its water and cover those losses. The next chapter discusses the many ways this assumption fails, but let's start with a typical example.

San Diego is a thriving city on California's arid coast, just north of Mexico. San Diego gets most of its water supply from aqueducts that were built over 50 years ago. The water from those aqueducts is sold at low prices that reflect delivery costs instead of the value or scarcity of water. Cheap prices encourage people to consume more, and the people of San Diego enjoy their water. Average daily consumption per person is around 600 liters (150 gallons) — double what someone in Sydney, Australia, consumes and five times an Amsterdam resident's consumption. San Diego's water managers worry about shortages, but they have not raised prices to lower demand. Instead they look for additional supplies.

About 20 years ago, they offered to buy water from farmers at a price that was twice the cost of existing supplies.

Customers did not find out how expensive that water was because managers averaged the costs of old and new water. Cheap water meant that scarcity crept up again, but managers did not raise prices. They decided instead to build a billion-dollar desalination plant.

Will the desalination plant "solve" San Diego's water issues? Not really. The plant will increase supply and increase costs, but those costs will not be clear to people who are paying $1.50 (based on the average cost of all supplies) for water that costs $2 to produce. The irony is that customers facing the real cost of desalinated water would probably reduce their demand by enough to make the desalination plant redundant.

Let's review. The cost of water supply depends on technology, plus the geography that changes the distance between water sources and uses. Higher prices can make it worthwhile to incur the higher cost of supplying more water. Each individual's demand for water depends on their preferences, or tastes. Tastes can include everything from a taste for showers to a taste for a big lawn. Changes in tastes will change how much water someone wants at stable prices. A rise in the price of water will not affect your taste for water, but it will tend to reduce the quantity of water you demand.

That is how supply and demand work separately, but their interaction depends on the number of suppliers and demanders in the "market." Competitive markets with lots of buyers and sellers — like markets for shoes or coffee — tend to exchange a variety of goods at reasonable prices without running out, but water is not usually allocated in those kinds of markets.

A monopoly manages scarcity — or not

Water is usually distributed by monopolies such as the utility delivering residential drinking water or government agency delivering irrigation water to farmers. Monopolies can pick their production quantities, qualities and prices without fear of losing customers because they have no competition. For some customers, their only choice is a bad one.

The monopolies controlling water supply have market power because it is difficult to find a substitute for water. This means that people are lucky when the water supplier sells good water at a reasonable price but unlucky when the monopolist sells cheap water to a few friends or runs short. Those bad outcomes will persist if the monopolist doesn't care about average customers or suffer in shortages.

How does one convince a monopoly to change its ways? The usual joke would end with "very carefully," but the answer here is known. Regulators and politicians can, in theory, tell monopolies to set fair prices that prevent shortages, but reality doesn't always turn out that way. Failures can result from lazy regulators, distracted politicians, stubborn managers, or a combination of all three. Outsiders will have a hard time understanding who is responsible for what, which makes it hard to allocate blame or target reforms.

I have dodged this complexity in Part I by assuming regulators, politicians and managers work to maximize public benefits. Part II delves into the tricky problem of selfish or inept representatives.

CHAPTER 2

Water on tap

Nobody wants to pay more for anything, but it is better to pay more for something than less for nothing. Sometimes we forget that value matters more than price.

In the good ol' days of abundance, it didn't make any sense to charge for water because it didn't matter how much people used. Utilities established to serve the public good did more good by delivering more water to people's homes, so they only recovered costs. More recently, they switched to volumetric charges to allocate delivery costs in proportion to use, but water was still free. That is why some utilities in arid places have lower water prices than utilities in wet places. It is as if they are selling gasoline at a price that includes the cost of delivery but omits the cost of oil.

Consider the desert city of Las Vegas and perpetually wet Amsterdam. Las Vegas gets fresh water from a nearby reservoir. Amsterdam takes contaminated water from nearby canals. High cleaning costs and durable infrastructure explain why water in Amsterdam costs five times its price in Las Vegas. Customers cannot see those differences, but they can see low prices, which is why each Las Vegas resident uses as much water as five Amsterdammers. People in Vegas have lawns and pools in the desert because water is cheap, but they also fear shortages. Water managers in Las Vegas have not countered that threat by raising the price of water. Instead, they subsidize the cost of removing lawns.

Yes, that's right. Water managers in Las Vegas sell water so cheaply that they pay people to *not* use it.

The end of abundance is forcing managers to face scarcity that their systems were not designed to handle. It is exposing costs and subsidies that customers were not meant to notice. After a short review of utility regulation, this chapter will explain how misplaced subsidies cause financial, social, economic and environmental harm. It concludes with an outline of how to price water in a way that reduces conflict, protects the environment, and keeps utilities financially solvent.

These solutions apply to managing water that is scarce in either quantity or quality. In both cases, we see that demand is greater than supply, the cost of scarcity is significant, and the games to avoid responsibility are creative. Proper pricing can end those problems.

Regulating public utilities

Public water utilities are called "public" because they have an obligation to deliver water to all households and businesses paying for service in their area. Municipal utilities are "public" in the sense that they are part of local government (*municep* means "citizen" in Latin). Investor-owned utilities (IOUs) are "private" in the sense that they chose their own management and operating procedures. Municipal and investor-owned utilities differ in ownership and profit-seeking, but those differences do not determine performance.

Customers have the most to gain in monitoring utilities to ensure a good balance between safe and cheap services, but they lack the time, expertise and organization necessary to do a good job. That is why they delegate that job to regulators.

Politicians or their appointees regulate municipal utilities. Bureaucrats from government agencies regulate IOUs. Both types of regulators want good service for customers, but they use different techniques. Municipal regulators often deal with water managers as peers in the same governance structure. IOU-regulators are government employees who interact with managers employed by shareholders. Both types of regulation can work smoothly or break down. Municipal regulators can use their insider status to help managers serve customers, but they may be a little too cozy to restrain managers from serving themselves. IOU-regulators can use formal hearings and benchmark indicators to drive utilities to perform, but they may also push inappropriate policies or ignore malfeasance.

Regulators want utilities to provide safe, reliable water service at reasonable prices. This target means that utilities and regulators try to balance between spending too much on gold-plated services that do not benefit customers and spending so little that water service is unsafe and unreliable.

Regulation also balances the interests of utilities and communities in a can't-live-with-you, can't-live-without-you relationship. Regulation reduces risk for both sides by trying to avoid extreme outcomes.

Regulations protect utilities by helping them recover their costs. Utilities must spend a lot of money on buildings, equipment and pipes before they can even sell a drop of water to customers. It can take over fifty years to repay loans against those fixed costs, so the regulator gives the utility a *legal* monopoly as the only supplier of household drinking water in its service area.

Utilities also have variable costs for energy, chemicals, some labor, and other spending that depends on water deliveries, but these costs are quite small relative to fixed costs. Water utilities average a fixed cost:variable cost ratio of approximately 80:20. Utilities providing power, telecommunications and other services typically have a lower ratio of fixed to variable costs, which means they are less reliant on debt, more flexible in updating facilities, and more capable of reducing their costs and capacity with changes in customer demand.

Regulations protect communities by preventing utilities from turning their fixed-cost burden into a threat. Say that a utility spends $80 to build a network that costs $20 to operate. That utility could charge customers $25 for water service to cover operating costs and repay fixed costs at a rate of $5 per year. The utility could also charge $40 without fear because another utility would have to spend $80 to build a network before it could even deliver water for, say, $30. No new utility is going to spend $80 for the chance to earn $30, but the old utility doesn't mind selling water for $30, $25 or $20 because it already has a network. Regulators limit charges to protect customers from a utility's *natural* monopoly power.

In theory, the regulator allows a utility to set its price at a sweet spot that is high enough to recover costs and deliver reliability but not so high as to harm consumers. In reality, the regulator may allow (or require) a utility to set prices that subsidize some customers or behaviors. Those subsidies distort decisions, disrupt performance and harm customers.

My subsidies are better than yours

... at least, that is what an old regulator told me. A subsidy for a good I like helps me consume more or pay less. Some subsidies are socially useful. Subsidized education, medical care or pensions help individuals *and* society. More important, they are fair because everyone can benefit from them at some point in life. Subsidies to special interest groups are neither fair nor efficient. A subsidy to tall people is unfair to everyone else.

Subsidies have existed in the water sector for millennia. Roman emperors subsidized the construction of aqueducts, bathhouses, and public fountains to show their power and improve public health. The modern era of sanitary sewers and drinking water services began when urban disease, fires, and filth threatened Paris, London, New York and other growing cities. Subsidized water services pushed these cities onto a sustainable, prosperous path.

People now understand the value of clean water and they are wealthier, so they are both willing and able to pay for adequate clean water. That is why subsidies should end in rich countries. (Chapter 7 discusses subsidies in poor countries.)

The next few sections explain how subsidies transfer money among customers, destabilize utility finances, and increase shortages. Don't worry about their interactions or relative impacts. You only need to understand how subsidies cause problems.

Subsidies from current users

Most cities build their water systems in phases, adding supply and extending networks to support growth. The private or municipal managers who run these systems usually set the same water prices for all customers. This "postage stamp" pricing means that customers on the old system pay as much for water as customers on the extended system. It also means that old customers subsidize service to new customers, which encourages growth and sprawl.

As an example, consider a town of 1,000 houses whose water supply comes from a well that cost $200,000 to drill and costs $20,000 per year to operate. Each household would then pay fixed charges of $200 to get connected and $20 per year for service. Now suppose that the city wants to add another 1,000 homes. Since the well cannot yield enough water to serve them, it has to build an $800,000 plant to extract and treat water from a nearby river at a cost of $80,000 per year. How much should the utility charge new residents?

Most water utilities set prices in proportion to average costs rather than the additional cost of service. Such cross-subsidies have existed for centuries, but their impact and cost has grown as cities have sprawled and utilities have turned to more expensive water sources. Some cities have kept postage stamp pricing to avoid introducing a new billing scheme or obscure the real cost of new projects. Others cities charge "impact" or "hookup" fees to offset new costs. Land developers, pro-growth politicians and businesses often lobby to minimize those fees because they care more about their profits from growth than the community's vulnerability to shortage.

Let's say new customers pay $800 to connect. How much should they pay for water? Proportional charges would mean existing residents would pay $20 per year while new resi-

dents would pay $80. That is not done with "fair" postage stamp prices in which everyone pays $50 per year and old customers subsidize new customers' burden on the system.

Some cross-subsidies make sense, but they should be minimized. Charges below the full cost of new service encourage excessive growth, unsustainable consumption, and unfair financial burdens. Customers should pay the full cost of connecting to the system, and they can if that cost is recovered over 20–30 years.

Subsidies from future users and outsiders

Water infrastructure is expensive and lasts for decades because it is built of durable materials strong enough to carry moving water. The disadvantage of long-lived, underground networks is that they are out-of-sight — and thus out-of-mind — to politicians and citizens. Invisibility may mean that insufficient funds are set aside for system replacement and repairs. Under-maintenance burdens future customers and decreases reliability for current customers.

Regulations can reinforce the problem. Utilities can make "rate of return" profits on their capital stock of machines, pipes and buildings. They are not allowed to profit from efficiency improvements that lower operating expenses, since cost savings must be passed to customers via lower prices. These rules mean a utility may prefer building new sewers to maintaining existing sewers.

Many water utilities also depend on grants, property taxes or foreign aid for income. Customers are probably pleased to pay less for water, but subsidies can destabilize finances and customer service. Managers listen to funders before customers. Politicians tell utilities to serve their priorities. Foreign donors demand equipment purchases from their home companies. A sudden departure of outside money can cause price increases that can lead to protests, water theft, unpaid bills, and service cuts. Employees may quit for easier jobs.

These problems can occur in poor countries receiving foreign aid and richer countries where water utilities are not run as self-sustaining, "corporate" enterprises. Many communities in the U.S., for example, ask for grants to upgrade wastewater plants to meet regulatory standards. But why should these communities get aid from other communities that have already paid to upgrade their wastewater systems?

What about subsidies to lower prices? Don't they help the poor? Yes, they might help some of the poor, but they encourage water use and distort the behavior of the non-poor, managers, businesses and others. The economic solution would charge everyone the full cost of water service and give income support to the poor. A compromise solution would subsidize some water for the poor. In Chile, for example, poor people get their initial water allocation for free but pay the normal rate for more.

This discussion is irrelevant in most countries, where people can afford to pay the full cost of operations, maintenance, replacement and growth. Sure, they would prefer to pay less, but maybe not if lower prices also mean lower reliability, outside interference and poor service. Water *consumers* who pay for water like they pay for food or clothes will be treated as *customers* deserving good service.

Subsidies from families

I recommend raising the price for *all* water in response to water scarcity, but many managers and politicians want to protect some people from higher prices. They do this with "increasing block rate" (IBR) water prices. IBRs mean that a household's first few blocks of water are cheaper than additional blocks (a block may have 1,000 liters or 1,000 gallons). IBRs supposedly protect the majority while penalizing "water hogs," but they are hard to get right. Managers set prices and blocks and hope that behavior generates targeted revenues. Customers usually do not know when they are using water from an expensive, higher block. The highest block price may reflect the theoretical cost of additional supplies but fail to prevent shortage. IBRs are also unfair because the number of cheap blocks does not usually reflect household size. It is easily possible for a rich playboy to pay less per unit of water than a poor family of five "water hogs" using more water.

Even ignoring all these problems, IBRs may not even reduce demand. Las Vegas's IBRs move very slowly from nearly free to ridiculously cheap. The first 600 liters per day (roughly 160 gallons) costs $0.20. The next 600 liters cost $0.40. Most people outside North America use about 100 liters/day/person, so a family of four Europeans in Las Vegas would pay 20 cents per day for their water, unless they want to fill their swimming pool. It costs $40 to buy those 55,000 liters (15,000 gallons) of water. Quite a bargain for a pool in the desert.

Water budgets supposedly improve on IBRs by awarding cheap blocks in proportion to headcount, land area, vegetation, altitude, temperature zone, and so on., but this "accuracy" brings complexity. Budgets are expensive to set and confusing to residents who need a spreadsheet to understand their water bill and telepathy to know if their neighbor's water use is fair. Even ignoring those problems, why should we give lawns the same priority as people?

Los Angeles, for example, allows someone with a large house and landscaping in Bel Air (postal code 90077, where the median household of 2.6 people earns $182,000) to buy 56 units of cheap water in winter and 90 units of cheap water in summer. A poorer family in a small house in East Los Angeles (postal code 90063, where the median household of

4.2 people shares an income of $39,000) can only buy 28 and 36 units, respectively, before facing higher prices. These allocations are the same for families of six or fewer people. It is neither efficient nor fair to give cheap water to playboys in mansions.

Simple prices — like the price of gasoline, coffee, wine or any other commodity sold by the unit — are easier for consumers to understand and use.

If water is scarce, raise prices. People will use less water, just as they would use less gasoline. Will higher prices threaten health and safety? We know — from studies and intuition — that people cut non-essential uses when prices rise. That is how we know people have plenty of water in the western U.S.: more than half of residential drinking water is sprayed outdoors.

Subsidies from heavy users

The cost of serving business and residential customers can vary substantially. It is cheaper to serve apartments near the treatment plant is cheaper than a mansion on a hill. A water bottling plant will use more water than a law office. Different costs should translate into different prices, but prices are often set in strange ways. Business customers pay more so homeowners pay less. Restaurants and offices pay more so governments and schools can pay less.

Lopsided prices distort behavior, transfer wealth, and skew competition. They do nothing to improve water management or customer service. They are likely to encourage groups to seek their own discounts.

Cross-subsidies get worse when utilities put more weight on variable charges than the share of variable costs might suggest. A typical utility has costs that are 80 percent fixed and revenues that are 80 percent variable. Under normal conditions such a scheme means that heavy water users subsidize light water users by paying a large chunk of everyone's fixed costs, but the revenues covering those costs can swing wildly if people buy more or less water. These cross-subsidies destabilize utility finances and management decisions.

Say, for example, that a utility charges a monthly fee of $20 against its fixed costs of $80 and charges $80 to deliver 10 units of water against its variable costs of $20. Now total revenue equals total costs, but what happens if it rains and demand falls by 5 units because people don't water their lawns? Fixed revenues and costs stay at $20 and $80, respectively, but variable revenues and costs drop by $40 and $10, respectively. Now the utility is making only $20 + $40 = $60 when it has costs of $80 + $10 = $90.

Most utilities try to cover this lost revenue by drawing on "rate stabilization funds," but these are often inadequate. Then they ask to increase volumetric prices, which angers customers who feel like they are being punished for using less water. Higher prices also induce customers to use less water, which further cuts revenue. Repeat this process enough times, and you will see the utility in a "death spiral" that culminates in public protests, lawsuits, financial games, and other distractions from supplying drinkable water.

Why doesn't the utility just raise its fixed monthly charges? That action would help stabilize finances, but it contradicts the utility's hard-won policy of using high water prices to encourage conservation.

Managers who depend on variable revenues also face mixed incentives. Higher consumption helps them cover fixed costs, but it also depletes water supplies. Decreased consumption saves water, but it reduces revenues. The Chief Financial Officer is going to get very mad, very fast if the utility is not selling enough water to repay its debts. Now you see why so many utilities say "conserve water" without *doing* anything to discourage water sales.

These confusing dynamics result from using one tool (the price of water) for two goals (covering fixed costs and reducing demand). They can be avoided by matching costs to revenues and *then* tackling conservation. The first step would mean raising fixed charges so customers pay their share of network capacity (larger connections pay more). The city of Davis, California, has implemented such a pricing method

with an ingenious twist. Fixed charges are based on me-
ter size as well as water use in the prior year. This method
ensures that customers pay for their long-run and "peaking"
burdens on the network. It also gives customers an incentive
to use less water now to save money in the next year. An
increase in fixed charges means that variable charges must
drop (to prevent profits), but that drop weakens conservation
incentives. Davis hopes that customers will use less water
today to save money next year, but I would use stronger incentives. The next section explains why we need them now
and how they would work.

Subsidies from the environment and our future

In the Beginning was Demand, and water managers treated it
as sacred. Modern managers keep their supply-side bias for
several reasons. They associate growing consumption with
growing wealth. They prefer to drill wells than ask customers
to use less water. They are engineers who like to build things.
They need to maintain reliability as politicians invite more
people to use more water.

Supply projects benefit humans directly, but they can
weaken ecosystems. Americans and Mexicans, for example, take so much water from the Colorado River that it dies
before reaching the sea. The death of the Colorado River's
delta doesn't just hurt plants, birds and fish — it deprives
humans of the indirect benefits of a functioning ecosystem.

The most important fact affecting water management
across all sectors, worldwide, is the financial cost of raw water: zero. A utility pays a fee for its extraction permit and an
irrigation district files paperwork to divert water, but neither
pays for the volume of water removed from rivers, lakes or
underground aquifers.

As we have seen, most utilities set prices to recover their
system costs. A raw water cost of zero means that water is
free to anyone paying for delivery, no matter water's scarcity
or value. Free is too cheap when there is a risk of shortage.

The variable price of water service should include a surcharge when water is scarce. A "scarcity surcharge" should

be based on the value of water taken from the environment or tomorrow's supply. It should increase with scarcity and fall (or disappear) with abundance. The price of water might rise from $2 to $3 per unit in scarcity but fall back to $2 (the cost of service) when water is abundant. These changes can be pre-agreed and based on water conditions. A drop in the surface level of a reservoir, the count of sequential days without rain, or other objective factor can trigger pre-agreed price increases. Some electrical utilities already use signals and triggers like these.

Scarcity pricing is more effective when combined with visible signals. Most drivers know the price of gasoline because it is posted at every gas station and obvious when they fill up. Water users would be more aware of water scarcity if reservoir levels were printed in newspapers or posted next to highways — as they are in Australia. Consumers would connect scarcity and use if their water bills showed the relation between scarcity and prices, the news announced reduced supplies were triggering pre-agreed price increases, or their smart phones told them their consumption and charges every day.

The bottom line is that the price of water needs to include the cost of delivery as well as the "opportunity cost" of using water here and now that we may want there or later. Singapore's PUB utility, for example, charges more for water loaded on ships, since that water cannot be used, cleaned and recycled back into their system.

Sustainable flows of water and money

You have heard more than enough about subsidies. Let's look at how to set charges to balance supply and demand.

In conditions of water abundance, it is possible to charge a fixed price for water service that covers both fixed (capital) and variable (operational) costs. Fixed fees can be set differently for households and businesses, depending on the number of residents, size of the connection, or some other agreeable criterion.

Some communities prefer to allocate costs in proportion

to use, so they will need to measure consumption. Water meters provide that information, but they cost money to install, service, and read. Those costs can be included with other variable costs that will be allocated to customers in proportion to their water use. New variable revenues allow fixed charges to fall to cover fixed costs. The utility will now be matching fixed costs and with fixed revenues and variable costs with variable revenues, which will stabilize its finances.

Meters are necessary when water is scarce, but they can contribute to operational efficiency even when water is abundant. Customers on meters use 20–30 percent less water because they have financial incentives to reduce their demand and repair leaks that cost them nothing previously. Meters also change perceptions at utilities. A system leak is free when revenues do not depend on water consumption. It makes sense to repair leaks when they represent lost revenue. Reductions in water consumption and leaks also reduce other costs, such as the cost of energy for pumping and treating water and wastewater. In the longer term, lower demand reduces capital spending on supply sources, the strain on natural water sources, and the risk of having too little storage capacity.

But what's to be done if a utility matching fixed costs to revenues and variable costs to revenues still faces water scarcity? The typical response may be an education campaign to tell consumers to use less, but that option can be accompanied by scarcity pricing, which is, in fact, what happened in the early 90s in Santa Barbara, California.

After several years of drought, water managers were facing a shortage. They gave reservoir updates on the evening news and reinforced their message by increasing metered prices by 900 percent for heavy users. Some customers cut their water use to save money; others used less to help out. These complementary scarcity signals reduced demand by 50 percent, but the effort also changed perceptions. Prices fell and announcements ended after rains returned, but consumption in the "new normal" stayed at 60 percent of pre-drought levels.

Prices generate revenues and reduce demand, but they also give customers choices. A regulation on outdoor watering may annoy a granny with flowers. A desalination plant may annoy environmentalists. An education campaign is condescending to some and a waste of breath on others. A campaign to install low-flow toilets may install sparkling receptacles in unused second bathrooms. Prices send a direct signal at the same time as they accommodate many responses. Customers can choose *their* own mix of technologies and techniques. Some will take shorter showers. Others will install drip irrigation. Some will shower at work. Others will just pay more. A higher price for water, like a higher price for any commodity, allows people to choose how much water to use. Choice is a pleasant option compared to water shortages or tickets from water cops.

Managers also benefit from higher prices, since they do not need to control one behavior or serve a sacred interest. They just need to focus on the aggregate changes in demand that result from thousands of people making little choices.

It is relatively easy to set a price for water that covers the variable cost of service and add a surcharge to that price when water is scarce. Such a scheme will break even when water is abundant, but produce "profits" when surcharges are used. Profits can be refunded to reduce fixed charges using existing accounting systems. In November 2013, for example, the water utility of Pismo Beach, California, sold some excess water, spent some of the proceeds on improving water management and sent the rest to customers. Who doesn't like a refund check in the mail?

Reliable service and fair pricing

Utilities should collect fixed and variable revenues in direct proportion to fixed and variable costs so their finances are stable. All customers should pay the same volumetric prices to be fair. A surcharge can be added when water is scarce and demand needs to fall. Excess revenue from that surcharge can be rebated to each household — without respect to their water use — to ensure that the utility uses higher prices only as a temporary means of preventing shortage.

These ideas are summarized on the next page where duplicate crib sheets illustrate how utilities can price water services for fiscal and environmental stability. The figure shows how water costs usually arrive (left column), the way that water is typically mispriced (center column), and how to price water correctly (right column). The light grey areas show the lopsided impact of conservation: A 50 percent drop in use reduces variable costs and revenues by 50 percent each, but total costs fall by much less than total revenues because variable costs are a small share of total costs while variable revenues are a much larger share of total revenues.

Copy, snip and distribute these sheets at your next cocktail party. People love talking about *realistic* ways to live with water scarcity.

Correct pricing stabilizes finances, encourages conservation
and prevents shortages

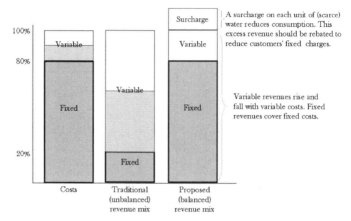

A 50 percent drop in use reduces variable revenues more
than variable costs (light grey areas) and destabilizes finances.

Correct pricing stabilizes finances, encourages conservation
and prevents shortages

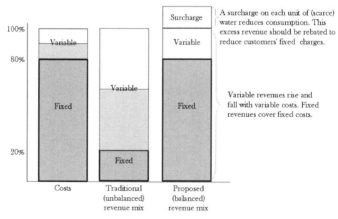

A 50 percent drop in use reduces variable revenues more
than variable costs (light grey areas) and destabilizes finances.

CHAPTER 3

Water for profit

I have met plenty of intelligent people who believe bottled water is evil, businesses waste water, the "energy-water nexus" must be managed, and private utilities exploit their customers. Their passion does not, unfortunately, allow for economic incentives. Let's see how money and water mix.

Don't blame the bottle

Bottled water is recently popular in rich countries, but it has always been popular in poor countries where people cannot easily get safe water. Why is bottled water popular with people who have access to good tap water? Some people prefer bottled water to soda, juice or other store-bought drinks. Others buy bottled water for its convenient container or to look cool. Lots of people prefer the taste of bottled water to tap water. There is nothing wrong — economically — with these choices. They come with the same costs and benefits as other consumer choices.

Taste and convenience aside, bottled water is controversial for the costs and benefits that consumers do not consider. These touch on plastic bottle waste, water quality, the impact of bottling on aquifers, and sustainable utility services.

Most bottled water comes in plastic bottles. These bottles — like the bottles in which we get Coca Cola or Pepsi — are usually recycled, incinerated or buried in sanitary landfills with other bottles. The problems start when plastic bottles end up on beaches, in lakes or along roads — spoiling the scenery, polluting the environment, and killing animals. That problem can be reduced by regular cleanups, but it can also be reduced by putting a deposit on bottles, so people get paid to collect them. Deposits work all over the world, and they can work for plastic water bottles.

Deposits can even fund a recycling scheme, by using part of the initial deposit to subsidize the cost of melting and reusing bottle plastic. Despite the benefits of this solution, the bottled water industry opposes deposits because deposits raise retail prices and lower sales.

Some people choose bottled water over "perfectly good" tap water because they do not trust the quality of their tap water, grew up with polluted tap water, or believe advertisements proclaiming "Bottled Brand X" will save their family. A ban on advertising will not remove those fears, but a side-by-side comparison of bottled and tap water quality would help consumers. Average consumers cannot detect contaminants in one-part-per-billion concentrations so independent agencies or consumer groups should test bottled and tap water for quality. Information would help utility managers and bottled water sellers compete, which would help consumers.

Can water bottling facilities deplete springs or groundwater? Yes, they can (and they have) but not automatically. Bottling facilities, industrial plants, brewers, agricultural irrigators, and urban utilities can be licensed and regulated to ensure that users do not harm each other or the environment. There is nothing unique to bottled water that makes this outcome more or less probable. The answer depends on the regulatory regime and property rights — topics discussed in the next section.

People who think bottled water threatens household water service come to their conclusion in three steps. First they say that different entities regulate tap and bottled water. That may be true in some places, but it does not necessarily affect safety. Second, they worry that bottled water sales reduce sales by water utilities. This objection doesn't register in terms of volumes of water or money; bottled water costs more per unit, but people buy much less of it. A third concern is that customers who buy bottled water will ignore tap water quality and thus allow managers to escape oversight. That concern is condescending, illiberal and illogical. It assumes that people will not care about brown water at their taps, that bottled water drinkers should be forced to drink dirty water, and that customers can force managers to do their jobs. Customers can certainly complain about managers, but regulators are the ones charged with ensuring utilities deliver good quality water.

Profiting from water

There is an astonishing difference between the prices of bottled and tap water. A liter of bottled water may cost $4 while the same amount of tap water costs less than a cent. Why doesn't everyone go into the bottled water business? Because "water" only accounts for a small share of the costs of getting a bottle into consumers' hands. The expense of packaging, transporting, and managing the supply chain eats into profits, and those profits are further squeezed by advertising in a competitive marketplace. It is hard to bottle your way to wealth.

What about businesses that use water to make money? Water's unique physical characteristics lower the cost of manufacturing everything from silicon chips to potato chips. Businesses use water to wash people's hair as well as their dishes. Offices need water to keep their employees happy and healthy. Should these businesses pay less for their water? Some governments claim cheap water creates jobs and generates taxes.

This is rubbish. All businesses try to minimize expenses and maximize revenues. Those that still lose money should shut down because their costs exceed their value to customers. Cheap water may help a business stay open, but it won't make a bad product good, compensate for poor service or contribute to employee pensions. Cheap water only results in more water use.

Businesses should pay the full cost of clean water —

including the cost of scarcity — and the cost of cleaning wastewater. These costs may vary by source (river, aquifer or utility pipe), but they should be the same for everyone.

Let's back up to the bottled water example, where I said that various water users might deplete an aquifer, river or reservoir if regulations or property rights are weak. Overuse and depletion can happen if the price of water is so low that demand from households and businesses exceeds supply. Neighbors who joined Club Abundance now find themselves fighting for their "fair" share of scarce water. Their utility can avoid shortages by directing demand to special customers, depleting supplies, or increasing prices.

Preferential access feeds corruption and inefficiency. Depleted reserves leave no water for emergencies or the future. Higher prices annoy businesses claiming cheap water makes jobs and individuals claiming a right to cheap water, but higher prices prevent shortages. That is relevant to businesses that want their doors open and individuals who prefer tap water to bottled water alternatives at one hundred times the price.

We know that higher prices can balance supply and demand to prevent shortages, but what about depleting aquifers and rivers? Those sources may be over-exploited (as common pool goods), but they can also be transformed into private or club goods. The private good route divides a known quantity of water among claimants. This is what happens when parents divide a cake among children to prevent messy fights. The club good route puts everyone who deserves access to water in a group that sets rules for sharing the water. Genesis 29:3, for example, describes how a shepherd could only water his flock with the agreement of others because the shepherds had placed a large rock over the mouth of the spring that could only be moved with help.

This example, which also appears in the Torah and Koran, demonstrates the common foundations of sustainable water management as well as the durability of rules suited to local conditions. Sustainable rules protect communal resources from individual predation.

These simple examples are not exhaustive. Thousands of regimes are operating around the world. The ones that balance demand and supply endure because they promote sustainable water use, which means that they allow traditions and activities to continue indefinitely.

Pay for energy, pay for water

The energy industry uses water to produce and distribute its products. Dams generate energy from falling water. Fracking uses water to free oil and natural gas. Biofuels use water to grow crops. Solar farms use water to keep mirrors clean and run steam turbines. All of these uses deplete or contaminate water in some way. All of them can use more technology to clean and reuse water. Even dams can be replaced by "in stream" turbines that generate power without stopping water flows. These technologies are expensive compared to "free" water, but their advantages grow with water scarcity — a status whose existence may depend on your perspective.

Water wonks say that "consumptive" diversions reduce the quality or quantity of water. They define the oxymoron of "non-consumptive use" as a temporary diversion of water that returns later. Some people claim that diversions to cool power stations or impoundments behind dams are non-consumptive, but biologists disagree. Power stations do not usually alter volumes by much, but they can return fatally hot water to natural bodies. Dams change the timing of water flows, confuse ecosystem inhabitants, and interrupt the evolution of a river's shape (its geomorphology).

Dams also increase evaporation by holding water in reservoirs. Lake Nasser, the desert reservoir created by Aswan High Dam, loses roughly 12 cubic kilometers of water each year. That quantity — over 20 percent of Egypt's water supply — works out to 400 liters per Egyptian per day. Those losses are unacceptable when forty percent of Cairo's 17 million inhabitants receive tap water for fewer than three hours per day.

It also takes a lot of energy to collect, clean and distribute water. A desalination plant uses energy to filter or evaporate water. Wastewater treatment uses energy to pump water though ponds and filters. Pumps use energy to pull water from underground, push it over hills, and pressurize taps in tall buildings.

The combination of carbon awareness and water scarcity has resulted in an entire industry of energy-water-nexus consultants who promise to optimize the joint production and use of energy and water. These consultants may be wasting clients' time and money by focusing on a small part of a larger system. They define efficiencies in tons of water, kilowatt hours or operational expenses while ignoring capital costs for equipment that can raise or lower efficiency. They ignore other inputs such as chemicals, cement, labor, land and ecosystems. They look only at a few links in the supply chain. It doesn't make sense to optimize energy consumption at a water treatment plant while ignoring household water heaters or irrigation pumps.

Nexus discussions thus miss the forest by focusing on a few trees. This mistake cannot be overcome by including even more data — the food-water-energy-climate nexus! — as these complex systems combine billions of individual decisions and interactions into outcomes that cannot be reverse-engineered into a single "decision function" for policy makers to understand or manipulate. Emergent behavior is full of noisy, contradictory signals that change for many reasons. It is better to step back and squeeze inefficiency from each sector with simple economic tools. A higher price for scarcity will nudge people towards using less water (or energy), each in their unique way.

Realistic prices will push some factories to spend extra money on machines that use less water. Others will use more water with machines that use less energy. A power plant may use a lot of free water for cooling, but it will recirculate and cool expensive water. A dam operator will not hold water for irrigators when shipping companies will pay to increase water depth in a river. Frackers will use massive volumes of water if farmers sell cheaply, but they will clean and reuse expensive water.

Water users should pay the full price of the energy they use, and they often do. Energy users should pay the full price of water, but they often don't. That is why water shortages are more common than energy shortages. Politicians may prefer to keep water prices low so that energy is cheap, but their short-term focus may cause long-term harm. Appropriate prices for water will eliminate the need to talk about a nexus.

Regulation drives success or failure

Most water utilities are in business for the long run because they have a monopoly over a group of customers who cannot buy water from another company. I mentioned in Chapter 2 that these utilities can be owned by governments or investors. Many people confuse this "public" or "private" structure with good or bad outcomes, but they oversimplify. Private and public utilities fail or succeed in different ways.

An investor-owned utility aims to produce a profit, but it also has the potential to import ideas from other locations, an incentive to improve efficiency, and a reason to find new customers. A public utility focuses on maintaining low prices, keeping staff happy, and avoiding risks that invite political intervention. Both types may underinvest in maintenance that has present costs and future benefits, and both know more than customers or regulators about their operational efficiency. Among economists, there is no theoretical reason or empirical evidence that clearly favors one ownership type over another. Private or public utilities can fail their customers due to poor or corrupt management, weak oversight, missing information, or some other reason.

Regulators can force monopolists to work towards price or performance outcomes that matter to consumers, but most regulators focus on inputs and outputs such as energy consumption or water deliveries. Ofwat, the regulator in England and Wales, stopped asking for "June returns" — thick reports with endless data — in 2011. Now Ofwat puts more weight on 20 indicators, although some ("post-tax return on capital") still focus more on profits than service. I'll describe

how benchmarking can improve utility performance and customer service in Chapter 6.

Profits yes, shortages no

Plastic water bottles are fine, unless they pollute the environment. Businesses can use as much water as they want if they
pay full cost. The water-energy nexus will not need to be
managed — or even understood — when water and energy
prices reflect scarcity. The private or public ownership of
the utility is not as important as a regulator's professional-
ism when it comes to serving customers.

CHAPTER 4

Recycled water

Few people like the smell, sight or thought of human waste. The same goes for dirty dish water, runoff in street gutters, and the tailwater of factories, farms and landfills.

Most of us consider dirty water useless. We even pay to see it flushed away. But increasing water scarcity is turning dirty water into a valuable resource.

We have been recycling water for a long time. Poor families share bathwater that is expensive to haul and heat. Systems that divert greywater from the sink to the garden save water and money. Hungry farmers use grey- and black (toilet) water to irrigate crops because death is a greater threat than disease.

Engineers and scientists have worked for centuries to find better ways to clean water. They employ deeper wells, smaller filters, stronger chemicals and smarter sensors to detect, remove and neutralize contaminants. The cost of removing contaminants falls when technology and techniques advance and rise as we use more and stronger chemicals.

The economics of wastewater are changing. In the past, it was cheaper to take fresh water than reuse dirty water, but times are changing. Stronger water quality regulations have increased investment in treatment technology. Increasing freshwater scarcity has raised the cost of clean water. The combination of cleaner wastewater and less freshwater has increased the attraction of recycling treated wastewater

into drinking water systems.

Wastewater is now recycled on a large scale in Australia, California, Israel, Singapore, and other places facing water scarcity. "Toilet to treatment to tap" is cheaper than desalination because there are fewer salts to remove and infrastructure connections are easier. There is no need to locate next to an ocean or drill into a deep brackish aquifer. Recycling is possible anywhere people flush the toilet. The only drawback — as any desalination lobbyist will tell you — is recycled water's flushed origins. The good news is that this "sin" is neither grave nor unique. Properly recycled water is very pure. I drink it.

It is interesting that people tend to reject recycled water from a pipe while pretending "natural" water is pure. They are often wrong, as almost all raw water comes from contaminated surface and ground sources. Londoners, for example, drink Thames River water that has passed through seven toilets. Luckily for them, it is cleaned once more before arriving at their taps.

The changing costs of cleaning water will disrupt our sensibilities and habits. People will drink bottled water in places where it is too expensive to remove pollution from raw water. Urban utilities may provide "three streams" of services: bottled water for drinking and cooking, tap water for washing and cleaning, and grey water for irrigation. New technologies may lead other cities to replace city-wide systems with neighborhood systems. The old paradigm of drinking water from one source and wastewater disposal at one sink may be replaced by closed-cycle, neighborhood systems. Independent, linked tap-to-toilet-to-treatment-to-tap facilities would lower risk through redundancy. These changes will challenge the one-size-fits-all perspective of the monopolist. Diverse inputs, outputs and policies will improve services to communities and reward creative managers who perform.

Balancing water accounts

We often forget that we neither make nor destroy water as it passes through our hands and bodies and circulates in the hydrological cycle. Precipitation flows into oceans, sinks underground, or freezes in place until it evaporates again. Water quality changes during this cycle as water touches different substances. Humans have learned to speed up the cycle — we make snow, boil tea, reuse wastewater, seed clouds, and pump water from ancient aquifers — but we affect only some water. The Sun drives most of the water cycle.

Water accounting can consider these large cycles, but it often focuses on a small, local portion of total water flows.

Farmers with plenty of water can flood their fields without worrying about waste or overflows. Farmers are more careful when water is scarce or expensive. Their reduction in waste looks good in local accounts, but it prevents water from "showing up" in the accounts of downstream neighbors, aquifers, and springs. Water accounts have always balanced, but we have been watching only some of them.

As an example, consider what happens when people conserve water by taking shorter showers, installing low-flow toilets or reusing their greywater. In some parts of the world, this conservation saves water, energy and money, but it can also reduce the performance of sewers and treatment facilities designed for less-concentrated sewage. A utility managing drinking water and wastewater will balance between physical conservation and financial performance, but balance is harder when these services are divided. Conservation at a drinking water company may translate into higher costs for its wastewater neighbor. The next section examines the wastewater company's options.

Charging for residential wastewater

In Chapter 2, I recommended that water services should match fixed prices to fixed costs and variable revenues to variable costs. A surcharge on water use would dampen demand in times of water scarcity. Wastewater service charges should follow a similar pattern, with modifications to reflect the fact that wastewater systems have a higher proportion of fixed costs, are usually not metered, and handle different quantities of contamination.

The combination of high fixed costs and missing meters means that most wastewater systems are now funded by fixed charges on users or property taxes. In some places, local governments or outside funders pay the cost of wastewater because the systems are "too expensive" for users or public health justifies a subsidy. These reasons should be weighed against the problems of outside interference that we also discussed in Chapter 2.

Fixed charges must vary if different users impose different burdens on the system. Residential and industrial users should probably pay different charges. Large industrial and commercial users can be metered for flows. Dirtier facilities such as food processors can pay a surcharge for heavier loads, but toxic releases should be cleaned on site. These policies are already used in many countries. They should be adopted in places where wastewater treatment costs are rising faster than revenues.

Now we need to decide whether residential users should pay a flat fee or pay in proportion to their discharges. Proportional charges, assuming similar contamination in flows, imply that charges should be volumetric. These charges can be based on incoming, metered drinking water, but some people want to deduct outdoor use, so that people are charged only for indoor water use that ends up at the wastewater treatment plant. This idea makes sense until you think a little. Does outdoor use have no effect on water quality?

Residential irrigation produces runoff that ends up in storm sewers. It also seeps into groundwater. In both circumstances, the excess water is often contaminated by chemicals and pesticides since homeowners often use "just a little more to make sure." The high cost of capturing and cleaning these non-point sources of pollution implies that outdoor use should count in some way.

This reasoning makes it easy to fall back on the simplest suggestion: set wastewater charges according to metered drinking water demand and use those revenues to capture non-point runoff, clean piped wastewater, and protect natural water sources from pollution. The same advice applies to industrial water users (as mentioned above), but even "the innocent" may need to pay more. Golf courses and parks should not get a break on wastewater charges unless they clean their runoff and protect community groundwater.

Minimizing non-residential pollution

Most urban water users pay for their pollution because they are connected to a sewerage network. Non-point sources are harder to identify or charge when discharges flow to a common landscape. It is difficult to identify which farm drained excess nitrogen into a nearby river, which mine leaked cyanide into an underground aquifer, or which street washed oil into storm sewers.

Volumetric wastewater charges can pay to clean some non-point pollution but people may object to using these charges to pay for stormwater capture and treatment. That is why separate stormwater charges should be based on surface area. City authorities in Berlin and Philadelphia, for example, charge property owners for the precipitation that runs off their land. These charges are reduced if owners capture stormwater for on-site reuse or groundwater infiltration.

Regulation can be more effective than prices at reducing toxic, non-point pollutants. A regulation may prohibit a chemical from being sold, dictate use in a designated area, or

require special treatment. Regulations may require recycling
of paint and used oil or on-site wastewater purification to remove contaminants that would exceed the treatment plant's
capacity. Zero-discharge facilities typically evaporate water
and solidify residues in an inert form that is easier to dispose
of safely.

Regulating multiple polluters

How does one maintain the quality of water in a river con-
taining runoff from multiple facilities? The usual goal is
to limit total contaminant loads, maintain dissolved oxygen
levels, and so on, but it can be hard to allocate load shares
among dischargers.

For this problem, I propose a "do no harm" regulation
that requires downstream water quality to be at or above its
upstream level. This can be implemented without monitoring by requiring a city's drinking water intakes to be below
its wastewater outfall. Such a configuration would be expensive in the many cities where engineers use gravity to move
water from a higher intake point to a lower discharge point,
but a "virtual system" could be installed using cheap sensors
that would signal if downstream discharges are dirtier than
upstream withdrawals.

Markets among polluters

Another solution allows big polluters to trade pollution rights
among themselves as part of a local cap and trade regime
that sets an overall level of pollutants for all or part of a
watershed, distributes pollution permits to dischargers, and
then allows them to trade permits. Cap and trade often
works better than regulation because it gives dischargers the
freedom and incentive to find cheaper ways to reduce pollution. Polluters with low cleaning costs can sell their unused
permits to others for whom pollution reductions are expensive. Cap and trade requires point-source measurement of
discharges and enforcement to ensure that total discharges
stay below the cap.

A cap and trade program in North Carolina has encouraged developers to restore nutrient-cleaning ecosystems so urban expansion did not further reduce water quality. A similar program for New Zealand's Lake Taupo has allowed a local trust to pay farmers to change their practices and therefore reduce nitrogen loads in a water body cherished by New Zealanders. These programs take time and effort to establish. Stakeholders may take a decade to agree on legislation and establish regulatory mechanisms — but they can improve and maintain water quality more effectively than regulations.

Politicians prefer to give away permits (often based on past emissions), but auctions would generate revenues instead of windfalls for polluters. Auctions would also reduce pollution quickly because polluters would have to pay immediately instead of just turning in their free permits. Where should auction revenue go? Some people want to use revenues to reduce other taxes. Carbon taxes lower income taxes in British Colombia. Other people want the government to subsidize green technologies, but bureaucrats are bad at choosing winners. Subsidies also favor technology over techniques that may be more effective at reducing pollution.

I recommend using some revenue to clean up past pollution and distributing the rest to people living in the polluted areas. The combination of cap, cleaning and compensation will improve existing residents' quality of life and attract newcomers. The resulting "greenification" will increase the population living in a cleaner environment.

Collective solutions to invisible polluters

Now we get to the non-point sources of pollution that are separate to the naked eye but intermingled when it comes to determining responsibility. Agricultural fields discharge fertilizers and pesticides into surface- and groundwater bodies, creating "dead zones" in lakes and oceans. Aquifers can be contaminated by leaks from oil, gas, mining or agricultural operations. The usual policy for reducing non-point source pollution is to regulate or tax fertilizer or chemicals, but these actions can lead to politically unpopular reductions in food output. Setback regulation requires that landowners establish buffer zones to slow and settle runoff before it reaches communal surface waters. This regulation is easier to enforce, but reduces the amount of land in production.

A more promising regulation would impose a collective penalty on a group of farmers or oil riggers whose activities, taken together, exceed pollution limits. The regulation would create a positive incentive to perform by establishing a baseline for pollutant loads and assessing a deposit from every land user. That deposit would be returned only if total pollution remained below the target. This regulation solves the regulator's problem of missing information by shifting the burden of monitoring onto landowners who know who is doing what. It also makes it easier for neighbors to teach each other how to produce with less pollution.

Insuring against catastrophic pollution

Regulations, prices and penalties work when the cost of pollution can be included in the final prices of goods, but how should we deal with rare but costly pollution? Many mining, drilling and resource-exploiting activities create private benefits that will be overwhelmed by an accident. The cost of the 2010 Deepwater Horizon spill (in fines and compensation paid by BP) was one hundred times the value of the lost oil. Companies faced with heavy cleaning costs may declare bankruptcy. Regulations prevent some accidents but not all. A total halt to potentially polluting activities is unacceptable, so it makes sense to reduce risk and mitigate damages by requiring accident bonds or insurance.

An environmental-performance bond is a guarantee issued by a company that will pay a large sum of money to the government if operations produce exceptional pollution or the company fails to clean up a site. Although some companies meet their bonding requirement by transferring cash into an escrow account held by a third party, most issue guarantee letters that trigger in the case of an accident. These guarantees can be risky, since companies that pollute also tend to fail in other ways. Freedom Industries, for example, spilled toxic chemicals into the river supplying drinking water to Charleston, West Virginia, in early 2014. The company declared bankruptcy when it could not pay damages or cleaning costs.

Insurance works by spreading the cost of a disaster across many operations. The insurer collects premiums from many producers and uses that money to clean up when a few have accidents. Pollution insurers must be able to pay for expensive cleanups, and they are careful to set guidelines and require reports that reduce their exposure. In theory, their experience and financial responsibility prevents risky ventures, but reality will bite if guarantees are too low.

The price of bonds or insurance should reflect the cost of completely cleaning a spill or site, taking care of injured people, and compensating for deaths. The price will be high when the operator has a poor reputation or the project is risky, but that is the point. Governments that exempt operators from adequate guarantees only shift risk to taxpayers. Even worse, they also transfer responsibility to a government that may not be equipped to handle disaster. I hate to think of how much more oil would have spilled if the U.S. government's Hurricane Katrina team was sent to deal with the Deepwater Horizon spill.

Insurance contracts or bonds may not work if it is necessary to allocate blame among multiple companies. It may take more time to figure out who pays what than clean up the site. Contracts should designate a default payer to minimize delay and damages. That insurer can find co-payers after cleanup begins.

Each of these issues is present in Alberta, Canada, where companies use a lot of water to extract crude from massive oil sands deposits. Alberta's provincial government requires that companies post performance bonds against the cost of cleaning up after they complete operations, but the government allows companies to guarantee those costs on a pay-as-you-go basis. This means that cleanup costs are not funded until projects are complete. No projects have ever closed, and only one tailings pond (Suncor Pond 1) has ever been reclaimed. Its polluted water was transferred into a neighboring pond.

The province's optimism is not an accident. Companies are not required to post bonds or buy insurance against pollution that occurs *during* operations. It is assumed that companies can and will clean up spills and compensate victims. That assumption was justified with the Deepwater Horizon spill, as BP was able to raise $40 billion in compensation, but the BP case was lucky (in a perverted way). Failures like that of Freedom Industries are more common. We should not give the benefit of the doubt when pollution can cause massive harm to people and ecosystems. Companies need to choose between fully insuring their risks and not operating.

Clean water worth paying for

Better technology, a social desire to protect the environment, and rising freshwater scarcity increase the benefit of recycling wastewater. Residential users should pay for the cost of cleaning wastewater and dirty urban runoff in proportion to their drinking water use. The cost of stormwater systems should be recovered from charges to landowners who let water run off their property. Industrial and agricultural pollution can be reduced through regulation, cap and trade markets in emissions, collective responsibility, or insurance against dangerous spills. Choose whatever policy you want, as long as it protects innocent people and the environment.

CHAPTER 5

Food and water

Farmers need cheap water to protect us from foreign food of dubious quality, maintain the rural backbone of our culture and feed billions, right?

Not really. Most farmers in developed countries are businessmen who provide food of appropriate quality to the highest bidder. Small-scale farmers are likely to maintain strong relationships in their communities, but commercial-scale farmers have a stronger relationship with their spreadsheets than the greens in your salad.

The contrast between romance and reality is not as strong for farmers in developing countries, but their reality is likely to be bent into tragedy by mismanaged supply chains, corrupt bureaucrats, and distorted markets.

All farmers turn water into money, and farmers — users of about 70–80 percent of the water in most countries — lose big when water runs out. Those high stakes explain why farmers complain when they do not get enough water, why they are increasingly in conflict with cities, environmentalists and each other, and why they lobby for relaxed enforcement of rules that "threaten food security."

I won't debate these claims as much as resolve them with this book's strongest policy recommendation: farmers must buy and sell irrigation water in markets if we are to save communities, maximize food production, and improve water management in other sectors.

This recommendation doesn't mean that all rural communities will thrive. Some will shrink and die. It does not mean that food will be cheap, everywhere. Some people will have to pay more. It does not mean that all agricultural and environmental demands will be met. Some farms and some rivers will go dry. My recommendation is aimed at maximizing the private and social benefits we get from water. It doesn't deny facts, but it does improve on them.

The right to scarce water

The agricultural revolution began about 10,000 years ago, when people saw that it was possible to grow more food when seeds were planted and watered. The revolution took a huge step forward when farmers figured out how to extract water from rivers, lakes and underground aquifers. Improvements in irrigation techniques and technologies brought more water at appropriate times, leading to further increases in yields.

Irrigation requires land, water, and infrastructure connecting the two. Infrastructure has been expensive and difficult to build for most of human history, but technological advances have made it easier to irrigate nearly anywhere. The problem now is that there is not enough water to fill all those dams and canals.

Water scarcity has increased the value of water, but water management decisions often ignore that fact. Irrigation districts, water user associations, and other entities charge farmers a "water price" that covers some costs, but other costs are subsidized. Subsidies enrich farmers and special interests such as agricultural suppliers, processors and traders, but they also distort land- and water-use decisions. That is how we get dairy cows living in air-conditioned tents in the desert.

What about the cost of water? It is often zero because farmers have water rights.

There are three main classes of water rights. The oldest rights treat water as a club good, in that all claimants are allowed to use as much water as they want, as long as their use does not affect others. These rights are often attached to land adjacent to rivers, where they are known as riparian rights.

Fun fact: rival is derived from *rivalis*, the Latin adjective for a person who shares a river (*rivus*) with another.

Riparian rights keep rivalry in check until water scarcity transforms water into a common pool good in which one person's use reduces water available to others. Those circumstances lead to the creation of a second class of right that allows its possessor to take a known quantity of underground or surface water as a private good. This quantified and exclusive right is often specified as "first in time, first in right" because it gives seniority to the first person to divert water in an act of "prior appropriation." Note that first does not always mean best. Prior appropriation rights require "beneficial use," but they do not — wisely — require highest and best use, which is very difficult to know or calculate.

People talk all the time about the value of water, but it is really hard to know one's own value, let alone someone else's (truthful) value. This problem extends to most goods and services we consume. Economists talk about our "demand" for these goods, but we cannot actually measure the values that drive demand. Instead, we assume that people place a higher value on the goods they get than the money they pay. The implication is that prices ration goods to the people who value them more.

This logic explains why markets increase happiness. They reshuffle goods and money among buyers and sellers so that both sides are better off. Buyers get something whose value exceeds the price they pay; sellers give up something worth less to them than the money they receive. Markets for irrigation water work in this way. Chapter 10 addresses the more complex question of valuing and allocating environmental water.

Private rights of prior appropriation eliminated overlapping claims through exclusion, but they created a new problem of exhaustion. Government policies encouraged people to use water instead of letting it flow, "wasted," in the environment. The appropriation of environmental flows for private uses resulted in drained lakes, dry riverbeds, dead springs, and a decrease in "public good" benefits that had belonged to everyone. Most of us are familiar with these disasters: The Aral Sea is dying as its source rivers are diverted into cotton fields. The Colorado River's waters nourish alfalfa fields and suburban lawns. Other rivers — Pakistan's Indus, China's Yellow and Australia's Murray, for example — turn to dust before reaching their deltas.

The value of environmental flows is obvious. Numerous cities were founded on rivers that provided water, transportation and beauty. Those rivers and other water bodies were abused for centuries before damages started to upset people, and a third class of right was created: a "public trust" right that reserves waters for all to enjoy, without exclusion, despoliation or exhaustion.

It is appropriate to note here that a public trust claim does not cancel private water rights as much put them into their social context. Many countries distinguish between an individual's "usufruct" right to *use* water and the state's *ownership* of water. Public ownership means the state can reassign rights from private entities to the public trust when community needs (public goods) need to be protected or restored.

This review of different classes of rights clarifies their differences, but it also explains how rights have evolved to meet different needs and how rights need to evolve with local conditions.

The dramatic example of Owens Valley, California, illustrates this point. The story begins in the 19th century with farmers who claimed prior-appropriation rights to water from the Owens River and nearby aquifers. The combination of low population and high return flows to the river and aquifers meant that farmers were using the water *as if* they had riparian rights.

Los Angeles saw an opportunity in Owens's water, which could be used for additional growth. The city bought land and executed its right to export prior-appropriation water via the Los Angeles Aqueduct (built in 1913). Those exports depleted local groundwater, drained Owens Lake, and diverted local rivers that fed nearby Mono Lake. The city's actions were legal, but their impacts were excessive. In 1983, the California Supreme Court ruled that Los Angeles's exports were damaging Mono Lake. The court weakened Los Angeles's rights in favor of a public trust right to keep more water in the lake.

This example shows how rights can conflict with social goals, which we will discuss in Chapter 6. In the meantime — and in the spirit of Part I's emphasis on water as a private good — we will examine the easier question of how to manage private rights among farmers and others who want to use water as a private good.

Getting rights right

We already discussed how urban water prices should rise when scarcity dictates that demand must fall, but that mechanism will not work with farmers who have the right to take water. Farmers who self-supply from aquifers or adjacent rivers pay only for pumping. Farmers who get water from irrigation districts holding their rights in trust pay the cost of delivery but not the cost of scarcity. These cost-recovery structures mean that farmers in water-scarce regions may be moving themselves and their communities closer to shortage. Farmers and society would be better off with a stronger signal of scarcity.

Markets provide good signals. The price of water in a market would help farmers decide between using scarce water for crops and selling it to someone with a higher value. Markets are also better at managing scarcity than self-control or regulation. Farmers may have a hard time holding back when they or others can make big money pumping water from a shared aquifer. Regulation often fails because farmers fight to use "their" water or block enforcement of limits imposed from outside the community. Markets overcome these problems by aligning profits with sustainability. Farmers have an incentive to enforce limits that will increase the value of *their* rights.

We just discussed three types of rights, but we are discussing prior-appropriation rights now, which brings up the interesting question of how farmers get those private rights. There are two ways to allocate usufruct rights among individuals or groups. One distributes rights according to political criteria such as first in time-first in right, special group priority, equality for all, or some other factor. An economic distribution assigns rights to those who pay the most. Once allocated, rights can be reallocated in many ways. The most common method is in exchange for money, but neighbors could, for example, swap "water now for water later."

Note that water markets — unlike oil markets — will be local due to the high cost of transporting water. A 42-gallon (160 liter) barrel of oil is worth about $100. The same quantity of agricultural water is worth far less than one cent. Local water prices will depend on demand from farmers and other buyers, weather, and many other factors.

Let's stop to make three important clarifications. Rights are often assigned in a political process and then reassigned according to economic criteria. Political allocation can create windfall gains to recipients who pay little or nothing to get valuable rights. Economic redistribution moves water to its "highest and best use" in terms of cash value. This political-economic two-step means that water can be allocated according to political forces in an initial phase and then economically reallocated for efficiency.

Another important criterion is the way rights are specified. A permanent right gives the owner the right to receive an annual allocation (or flow) of water that varies from year to year. These allocations can then be used or traded. The price of a right is usually higher than the price of an allocation in the same way that the cost for buying a house is greater than the cost of renting it. It is for that reason that the price of rights fluctuate in a wider range, as their value depends on long-term forecasts of water supply, political decisions, neighboring claims, and so on.

Allocations may not arrive with the same regularity. Senior permanent rights with reliable annual allocations are worth more than junior rights that may be "dry" in water-scarce years. Traders in Australia's Murray-Darling Basin water markets sometimes see the price of allocations rise above the price of rights. "Dry" junior rights are not worth much when farmers need "wet" allocations now.

The final clarification is the most important because it must be decided first: how much water can be allocated? This basic question has often been ignored. Plenty of rivers have been allocated to the point of zero environmental flows. Other rivers are *over-allocated* such that some rights can never be delivered. This crazy result is a hangover from a past in which politicians issued rights without acknowledging physical limits. Their myopia may reflect the purchase of votes today for rights tomorrow, but it also followed from a belief that water was wasted if it flowed into the sea.

Past political decisions complicate efforts to restore environmental flows. Governments have found the process of nullifying or repurchasing rights to be slow, costly and controversial. Even the name ("rights") complicates matters in countries where property rights (no matter how acquired) are sacrosanct. Governments facing shortages often reclassify rights as "licenses" that expire after some time to make it easier to match changes in supply, demand and social priorities.

The other complication with "how much?" is defining the quantity of water at its supposed source. It is difficult to estimate the sustainable yield of an aquifer. Withdrawals should be less than recharge, but complex flows vary by time and place. Groundwater and riparian rights will interfere with each other when those rights legally separate flows that are physically connected. It is also difficult to quantify "how much" when water rights are defined in terms of diversion instead of consumption. We therefore need to discuss a farmer's "use" in terms of the original diversion, use through evapotranspiration, and the quantity and quality of tailwater returning to aquifers and rivers.

Say, for example, that five farmers — each with the right to divert 10 units of water from a river — "waste" water to the extent that half of their diversions return to the river. These numbers mean the five farmers divert 50 units of water but only reduce river flows by 25 units. Their consumptive use will rise if they switch to low-leak, high-efficiency irrigation equipment because they will be able to use all 50 units of their rights. Efficiency can dry out a river.

After so many caveats and clarifications it may be good to summarize. Luckily, I can borrow a resource management checklist from water expert Chris Perry:

Account for available resources

Bargain to determine rights and priorities

Codify rights and priorities into rules

Delegate implementation to appropriate agencies

Engineer the infrastructure necessary to deliver water

Feedback results to adjust steps A-E

We discussed A–D, with the caveat that details depend on local institutions. We will discuss infrastructure in Chapter 8, but we know already that infrastructure can impede or facilitate reallocation. Now F. Feedback is essential if we want to correct errors and adapt to changing conditions. Adaptation takes place by changing rights to account for environmental flows, regulating quality, improving accounting, and so on. Those methods are discussed elsewhere in the book. Let's discuss markets as a means of adapting now.

Markets for water

Today's distribution of water rights may not reflect or reconcile new and existing users' diverse valuations of water. The current distribution of rights may also fail to reflect changing social priorities. These observations imply that existing water rights or flows may need to be reshuffled.

Consider, for example, two communities of farmers in southern California. Farmers near San Diego grow avocado trees using water supplied by a regional water agency. Farmers to the east, in Imperial Valley, grow alfalfa, switchgrass, lettuce and other water-intensive crops using water from the Colorado River. The avocado farmers do not have senior water rights. Their water is expensive. Imperial Valley farmers with senior rights pay about one-tenth the price avocado farmers pay. These facts hint at big differences in water values and the potential benefits of reallocation when drought struck and supplies fell, but there was no market. We could have seen a shift of water from alfalfa fields to avocado trees that would have benefitted everyone. Instead we saw hundreds of dead avocado trees, bankrupt farmers, and traumatized communities.

This dramatic example illustrates only one way that markets can improve efficiency by moving water to higher value uses. A market can also be used within an irrigation district where people are retiring, shifting between annual and permanent crops (from corn to trees), or facing excess demand for limited supplies. They can reallocate water flows for one year or water rights forever. Regional markets can help cities share a river crossing their territories, governments purchase water to restore environmental flows, or industries reshuffle water portfolios among dams, factories and power plants.

Although some people think that political or bureaucratic mechanisms are faster or more effective at transferring rights to meet social priorities, many of these same people often fail to consider the legal and logistical complications of taking water from traditional users. Bureaucrats will have a hard time separating truth from embellishment among noisy supplicants and highly paid advocates agitating for priority. Farmers will like the opportunity to sell or rent their water to urban and industrial interests, but who sells at what price?

Markets can supply those answers, but they should only be used after allocating water to environmental flows (Chapter 10) within the context of Chris Perry's checklist. We need to know, in other words, how much water is available, who has the rights to that water, who oversees water allocations, and how infrastructure will permit or prevent reallocations. It may take a few years to clarify this information and establish appropriate institutions for reallocating water, but those steps are necessary if we want win-win markets.

The simplest "market" allows two neighbors to exchange water for money, future water, labor, or some other good.

A larger market can work in areas where numerous buyers and sellers trade water within a watershed or share infrastructure that allows deliveries at different locations or times. The market will work better with low transaction costs (the time and money spent finding a partner, negotiating a trade, and completing the deal). Transaction costs depend on local customs, laws and experience. New markets tend to have high transaction costs, so it is important to consider them when designing and implementing markets.

Spot markets allow buyers and sellers to make deals at various prices and volumes, but the benefits of flexibility come with costs in terms of low volumes, wide price ranges, and idiosyncratic trading partners. Auctions will outperform spot markets when a known quantity of water needs to be simultaneously allocated among 20 or more users with access to the same distribution system. These systems can be as small as an irrigation canal adjacent to 20 farms or as large as a river passing 20 cities. Auctions can respond to irrigation schedules, supply updates, or some other metric.

Auctions can take many forms, but I have come to believe that a single-price, pooled auction is most appropriate for reconciling different demands for water. This design has two advantages. First, it replaces truth, fiction and conjecture with a cash bid. Second, it makes it easy to allocate units of water to various bidders from a central pool of water (or rights) owned by the government or other water supplier.

A single-price, pooled auction allows multiple bids from each participant. The highest bids win units of water, but they all pay the same price, which is based on the highest losing bid. This is how eBay auctions work: the winning bidder gets the good but pays a price based on the second-highest bid.

Say, for example, that 20 people make 131 bids for 80 units of water. Bids are ordered from highest to lowest, the highest 80 bids win, and remaining 51 bids lose. Winning bidders pay the seller the same price for each unit of water that is based on the 81st bid. (Winners also pay delivery costs.)

A modification of this single-seller auction allows us to reallocate water among many owners of existing rights. These auctions are more complex because sellers approach the market with different goals and opinions. Some owners may not want to sell — or know they want to sell. Their lack of participation lowers the benefit of an auction by limiting the volume of water for sale. Other owners who place higher values on *their* water than they would offer as buyers may not sell. Non-participation and over-valuation prevent useful trades. These effects can be overcome by forcing owners to trade, but force is incompatible with a voluntary market.

A few years ago, I designed a forced market that was not an oxymoron. An all-in-auction (AiA) puts all rights (or allocations) into a pool and allows eligible parties to bid for that water in a single-price auction. The key innovation is that the proceeds of the AiA are distributed among those whose rights are auctioned. The AiA moves water to those who value it most without violating the rights of owners because owners can "bid for their own water" if they want to keep it. Any owner can outbid a billionaire for his own water because the owner's payment returns to him. A farmer, for example, can bid $1,000 for his water. If someone else bids $1,200, then the farmer can sell his water or bid $1,500, knowing that the price he pays to win will be matched by the price he receives as a seller, leaving him with his water and no change in cash.

AiAs should be matched to local conditions. Rights owners decide who can bid. Farmers may sell to outside bidders
(a city, environmental organization or irrigation district), but
those sales should be limited until everyone understands the
impacts of outside money and water transfers.

How would this AiA work? Let's say that Al, Bob and
Chuck each put two units of water rights into an AiA that
has 30 farmers bidding for 60 units of water. Each farmer
can make multiple bids, and bidding does not end until everyone is satisfied with their count of winning bids. This
"soft ending" makes it difficult for anyone to object that they
did not have a chance to buy as many rights as they "need."

Say there are 100 bids, including bids of $10 and $4 from
Al, $20 and $20 from Bob, and $15, $12 and $10 from Chuck.
An ordering of bids reveals that the 61st bid is $5, which
becomes the price of water in this sale. This price reduces
the winner's curse — paying more than others — as well
as establishing a public benchmark for the current value of
water in the community.

Water is then allocated to those making the 60-highest
bids, with each paying $5. A comparison of the price and
the bids from above means that Al buys one unit of water
and takes away $5, leaving with one less unit of water than
he brought. Bob buys two units, thereby buying back his
water. Chuck buys an extra unit of water, paying $5 as well
as buying his two units back.

Note that this market — like any other — can reallocate
permanent rights or temporary flows. (The use of flows,
like the use of a rented house, does not transfer ownership.)
I recommend starting with a market for flows because the
value of today's water is clearer than the value of a right to
receive water forever. Markets or auctions for water rights
can come later, if ever.

Markets allocate water to those who are willing to pay
more and deliver money to those who do not want the water
as much. Markets can be designed around existing rights,
infrastructure and institutions to ensure win-win trades, but
those benefits are not always obvious to everyone.

The challenge of change

I have discussed water pricing and market reforms with urban, agricultural and environmental interests. Usually they are desperate for a solution. Usually, I offer something that fits their local conditions. And usually they stay with familiar but dysfunctional traditions that feed lawsuits, upset people and deplete water.

Their inaction upsets me, but I can see their perspective. Risk-averse water managers want to know if others have gone first. If I tell them about the vibrant water markets in Australia's Murray-Darling Basin, then they want to know if someone in the U.S. has gone first. If I tell them about Colorado-Big Thompson's active market, then they want to know if someone has already marketed water in their state. The next answer doesn't really matter as it is easier to stick with the devil you know than risk blame from someone who experiences real or imagined harm from change. It would be easier to promote change if winners spoke out, but they often stay silent to avoid notice of their good fortune or attacks from groups that want free water.

Water managers also tend to mistrust prices that allow people to use as much water as they like or markets in which competing participants "discover" prices. Most managers are accustomed to setting a price and supplying every claim, even if that means running short on water. They may not believe higher prices will cut demand or like the idea of selling water to high bidders.

Larger, transparent markets can also threaten people who benefit from lopsided allocations and water values. Water brokers know who's looking, who's selling and what's available on the right terms. They earn big commissions on complex, infrequent deals. As a former real estate broker, I learned how middlemen will fight to maintain their information advantage and commissions. The irony is that buyers and sellers who think they can outsmart everyone else also support brokers. Their self-deception helps brokers more than water users.

Finally, there is often a missing political interest in implementing markets. Local politicians often prefer the risk of shortage tomorrow to constraints and reforms today. Regional and national politicians may assume that those with property rights know how to use them, but they ignore the social importance of moving water to better uses, the aforementioned cautious nature of water users, and the high cost of bailing out water users who run dry. Time after time, I have seen water-short farmers pleading for financial rescues because missing markets or outdated laws prevented them from buying water from neighbors with reliable supplies.

Everyone wins when farmers buy and sell

Water rights need to be reformed to reflect water flows, consumption and supply. Farmers will use less water if they can profit from selling it in markets that reflect local conditions. Markets for water flows are more flexible and less risky than markets for rights. Farmers have the most to gain from markets because they have legal or traditional rights to most water. Farmers have made billions from trading and reallocating water in Australia's Murray-Darling Basin. Oregon's Freshwater Trust has used markets to restore environmental flows and quality in many of that state's rivers. Those are just two examples of the many win-win possibilities of markets for water.

Part II

Water for *us*

CHAPTER 6

Water for the community

Go anywhere in the world and you'll find two opposing sides to a water allocation. A farmer complains about water going to the environment. An environmentalist complains about water going to the city. A businessman complains about water going to farms. All of them know *they* deserve the water more than others. All of them know politicians should allocate water to its highest and best use. All of them doubt the politician's judgment.

These perceptions explain why water allocations are both important and controversial. In Part I, we assumed correct allocations or described how economic mechanisms could improve on initial allocations. In this chapter, we look at how politicians affect allocations and water managers may fail customers, but description doesn't automatically lead to prescription. Everyone has a different view on how to serve the community; decisions and actions must reflect past decisions, present values, and future hopes. Managers and politicians will need help if they are to manage water in the community interest.

Don't wait for the philosopher king

We all have a vision of how to do things. Each of us claims to know the "right" density for housing, the "fair" price for an hour's work, and the "correct" amount of water to leave in a stream or put on a field. Unfortunately, we do not all realize

67

that our views may not align with others. Awareness of that difference is what separates idealists from pragmatists.

In an ideal world, a water manager would match demand and supply to make sure that water goes to its highest and best use, but that process implies knowledge of the value of water in residential, agricultural, environmental and other uses as well as knowledge of present and future supplies of water in different places. A selfless, brilliant public servant would find it extremely difficult to reconcile diverse values, present data and future changes. A typical manager facing a range of reasonable positions and actions could easily choose a path that reflects a comfortable bias over a nebulous community interest.

I am not trying to paint politicians, bureaucrats or water managers with the brush of corruption or incompetence. I am merely highlighting the challenge that any of us would face if we were told to manage water for the community. The challenge is not a lack of data as much as the subjective lens that each person brings to those data. Although it may make sense to recognize our biases and try to integrate others' opinions, that process is likely to be skewed by our experiences and others' forcefulness. An irrigation manager may neglect environmental water flows. A poor manager may ignore industry's plea for reliability.

Humans have wrestled with "social good" for millennia. Plato wished for the wise rule of a philosopher king. Theologians explained outcomes as the will of their particular god. Political economists and philosophers described how a robust constitution would leave citizens indifferent to power. The diversity of theories reflects the diversity of humanity.

We will not eliminate that diversity, but we can work with it in two steps. The first is to separate politics from economics. That is why I put economic water uses and policies in Part I. It is not necessary to use politics to manage private goods, just as it is not necessary for your mayor to know how long you are in the shower. Prices and markets make it easy to balance the supply and demand for private goods.

The next step is to allow for policies that are simple enough to protect common goods but flexible enough to allow a variety of behaviors. We must reconcile different views when it comes to managing common pool and public goods. The right answer for *your* community depends on the weights attached to opinions. Should a majority of 100 get agricultural irrigation if only 20 people favor the environment? Should I die for lack of drinking water to protect a dozen people from the inconvenience of shorter showers? Can we ask poor people to spend now for protection against future storms? These questions have an easy answer on each side, but we want the same answer on both sides.

A community can move closer to common answers by asking people to ignore their personal role, costs and benefits. An approach from "behind the veil of ignorance" will help people be pragmatic, creative and engaged. If nobody has the answers, then everyone can participate in the solutions. This metric is not a call for group hugs and kumbaya chants. It is a call for mutual respect and compromise in updating policies to reflect our changing values of water.

Monopolistic customer service

Think of how you decide what or where to eat. You may consider location, taste, cost, convenience, and other factors before making your choice. You also know that you update your beliefs or choices as you experience the consequences of your actions. Now think of a one-size-fits-all government policy that doesn't fit you at all.

Incentives and performance in competitive markets differ from those of monopolistic bureaucracies. We are generally happy with markets that provide lots of choices, but we play with chance when one guy is in charge. Politicians can ruin your life or make it much better. We depend on their talents and whims. Yes, there are checks on abuse and oversight on performance (more on those in a moment), but checks on poor political behavior don't work as fast or effectively as checks on poor market behavior. We can change restaurants a lot faster than we can change cities. We are similarly

dependent and ignorant when it comes to the talents and
choices of local water monopolists.

How do we get monopolies to perform? The easiest
way is put good people in charge of the monopoly so they
can serve the community. A good regulator can help, but
regulators do not usually know as much as they should.
Competition can push some under-performing divisions of
a monopoly to perform, but its core operations will remain
insulated. At that point, it may be possible to create virtual competition via benchmarking or performance insurance. All of these complementary options can be reinforced
by community involvement and oversight. Let's explore each
of these ideas.

Who claims the blame?

A regulator is responsible for pushing a monopoly to perform, but some regulators are lazy, corrupt, or captive to the
industry they are supposed to oversee. Regulators report to
politicians, but politicians will hesitate to intervene in the
utility's tangled relations among debt-holding banks, consumer advocates, unions, and other stakeholders. Regulation
works well when targets and actions are easy to monitor, but
regulators cannot know how a manager can or should act.

Water managers deliver results amidst a complex web
of staff decisions, regulatory obligations, and customer demands. Managers may choose to suit themselves or please
customers, but outsiders may never know which goal they
seek. It is hard to compare "unique" monopolies on performance. Managers may understand exactly what is going on
and make a self-centered decision or understand very little
before making a customer-oriented decision. Customers are
unhappy when a pipe breaks, but they will not know if it
broke as a result of bad work or bad luck.

I have been watching water managers for a decade now.
I've seen service failures, price increases and conflict over
scarce water. I have a hard time knowing whether managers
are doing their best in these cases, but I worry when failure
has no consequences. The Tennessee Valley Authority, for

example, spilled toxic tailwater into a river and destroyed homes in 2008. How did managers pay the resulting $1.3 billion in fines and cleanup costs? They raised prices for customers.

Professionals provide service

Those examples can break your heart and your wallet, but they are newsworthy because they are rare. Many of us should be thankful to have professional water managers who deliver good service under the supervision of diligent regulators. We should be thankful when our fellow citizens attend public hearings to clarify when policies fail community interests. We may be pleased to see our local water company compared to peers in terms of cost, quality and reliability in public reports that make it easy to link spending to outcomes.

This state of happiness is reality in countries like the Netherlands where water companies voluntarily rank their excellent performance, but it is fantasy in others. The absence of basic statistics does not indicate missing information. Managers know their operations. Customers do not know what is happening because managers and regulators have decided to spare them the burden of knowledge. Or perhaps they don't want customers poking around, asking questions that may force them to work harder.

Competition delivers service

The first path to good water service is a manager who is a motivated professional. The second path is an incentive structure that rewards or punishes managers for meeting customer goals. Managers with "skin in the game" will work harder. They will be diligent about water quality when they drink from the same tap. They will pay more attention when customers can choose a different tap.

It is easier to break a legal monopoly than a natural monopoly. Fixed-line telephone companies enjoy a natural monopoly from their wired network, but regulators who allowed mobile competition helped improve service and lower prices. A drinking water monopoly can be forced to compete on quality with bottled water companies (Chapter 3) as well as other non-networked services. Scotland has, for example, allowed firms to offer water service agreements to businesses. These new retail providers buy wholesale water service from Scottish Water's network and bundle it with their own customer service. Competition has improved service, an area aching for consumer-centric innovation.

Competition can take other forms to fit local conditions. Slum dwellers benefit from private water kiosks and outhouses. Contracts to build or service facilities can be awarded through competitive tenders. Bulk water can be allocated in a market rather than a bureaucratic "beauty contest."

These competitive reforms can only dig so far into a monopoly's operations before fragmentation jeopardizes the monopoly's integrity and service reliability. At this point, it is better to create virtual competition among similar monopolies in different places by comparing their performance to benchmarks. Price, reliability and quality comparisons will help customers — and managers — see if they are getting value for money.

Benchmarking may not capture the complexity of operations in which a staff of hundreds takes water from distant and underground locations, makes it "healthy" and delivers it through a network of pipes and fixtures to millions of customers. I have developed an idea for "performance insurance" to deal with the complex relations among those inputs, outputs and outcomes.

Performance insurance would pay for accidents and other failures the way auto insurance does. Its price — like the price of auto insurance — would reflect risk, as calculated by an underwriter with knowledge of operational excellence at water utilities. Well-run utilities would not have to pay much for insurance, but badly managed ones would.

A regulator must require insurance — offered by competing companies — to ensure that all utilities were being evaluated for risks and paying a fair price for coverage. Customers and regulators could add the prices of service and insurance to understand direct and expected costs, respectively. It is not possible to do that today, since a price comparison of two similar utilities clarifies only which has a lower cost, not which one is better run. A comparison that included the cost of performance insurance would clarify whether affordable prices resulted from good management or skimping on reliability.

Water prices in Copenhagen, for example, are nearly triple Barcelona prices. Are these differences due to local labor costs, water sources and infrastructure condition — or do they reflect risk and management? In 2008, Barcelona needed to import emergency water on ships and many people had to drink bottled water to avoid bad-smelling, foul-tasting tap water. Copenhagen water does not have these quality and quantity problems, so you decide if it is worth paying $5 for 1,000 liters of Danish tap water.

Who would profit from performance insurance? Insurance companies would obviously make profits, but they would do so in exchange for bearing risk and monitoring utilities. These actions would "profit" customers who would pay a little more per month instead of getting surprises and sudden price increases. Most of us have experienced this trade-off with auto insurance. We make regular payments to avoid the risk of big payments. Performance insurance represents the same trade-off, with the additional benefit of better performance from water managers who have the insurance company there to help them improve reliability. Insurers watch more carefully than regulators because "accidents" cost them millions.

A community takes care of itself

Markets and price signals can improve performance but non-market forces can also help. A community can run its water monopoly as a cooperative, form a citizen's watchdog council to professionalize community oversight, or make the utility more dependent on its consumers as *customers*. A utility that gets 80 percent of its financing from banks, governments or investors is more likely to pursue their priorities over consumers'. Consumers can also influence outcomes by participating actively in governance discussions and decisions. Community guidance and governance will turn passive consumers into active overseers, supporters, directors and customers.

But sometimes consumers are not invited or allowed to have a say. They may have to accept the service they are given. Politicians and bureaucrats with discretion may use their power wisely, but sometimes they make mistakes, follow their biases, or put their choice ahead of the public's choice. Unhappy customers have only three options: exit, voice or loyalty. Exit means leaving the area, which can be costly. Voice means complaining about service, which may lead to change or frustration. Loyalty means enduring and adapting, which will help you survive until you depart or luck arrives.

Luck arrived in 1993 when the Cambodian government appointed Ek Sonn Chan to head Phnom Penh Water Supply Authority (PPWSA). Mr. Chan turned a shambles into a world-class utility by sacking corrupt staff, collecting revenues from the army and other deadbeats, and expanding PPWSA's network to rich industrialists and poor slum-dwellers alike. Mr. Chan also multiplied his influence by attracting passionate staff and paying bonuses for good performance. PPWSA now has a culture of pride — and reputation for customer service — that gives staff, customers and politicians the expectation of future success.

I could tell many stories about other successful professionals, but this book is directed at the managers who need more help, better ideas or early retirement. Businesses change for fear of losing customers to the competition. Monopolistic water organizations face no such threats, so they change if and when they want. We must be patient with water managers and regulators who learned their trades in an age of abundance, but patience does not mean disengaged indifference. We need to engage them as customers who deserve good service. Tradition will burden consumers with higher bills, unreliable service, and a weakened community. Customer-responsive action will promote sustainable economic and social development.

CHAPTER 7

A human right to water

In Chapter 2, we went over the basic economics of utility water service, which is mostly concerned with charging enough to cover the long-run cost of service, keeping subsidies among users to a minimum, and signaling scarcity to customers. That discussion assumed managers want to do their jobs and customers can pay for water service, but those conditions do not always hold. This chapter discusses options in the absence of will or money.

People who claim a human right to water will deliver water to the poor often forget that it takes a functioning government — and a subsidy from rich people — to produce that outcome. The UN Committee for Economic, Social and Cultural Rights, for example, says governments "must establish that they have taken the necessary and feasible steps towards the realization of the right to water...a failure to act in good faith to take such steps amounts to a violation of the right." These words highlight the necessary role of government in delivering rights-based water services. They also clarify that the poor will need to find an alternative path to services if government is not interested in their rights.

In the previous chapter, we discussed how managers and politicians can serve themselves instead of the public. The lack of water services to many of the world's poor can be traced to the indifference of these "leaders." I came to this conclusion after I analyzed two sets of developing countries.

In the first set of 17 countries, governments had promised a human right to water, but that right was absent in a second set of countries with similar per capita incomes. I compared both sets to see if access to water services increased at a faster rate in countries with a right to water than it did in countries without rights. There was no difference.

This result is not too surprising. Rights only lead to results when governments are honest. Dishonest governments, on the other hand, do not care about human rights, legal promises, or citizen complaints. An honest government will make sure that citizens get good quality water because people do not want to get sick or die. Water service does not depend on rights. It results when a functioning government tests water quality, controls monopoly power, and so on.

Good governance (a lack of corruption) separates civilized countries from their dysfunctional, struggling neighbors. I tested that theory by comparing governance quality to access to water services in 162 countries. The strong, positive correlation between the two allows us to conclude that honest government and quality water service are usually found together.

This perspective can help us improve water services to the poor by reframing the debate in terms of governance and money instead of rights. Wealthy people with good government will get water service, but poor people with corrupt government will not. People will also get water service in the intermediate cases of good government with poor people or bad government with rich people. An honest government will help poor citizens get water. Rich citizens will get water whether or not the government is honest.

I would love to end right here by proclaiming honest government and wealth for all, but reality will not comply. We will spend the rest of the chapter looking at ways to help poor people avoid dishonest governments. We will begin with the "helpful" monopolies that set prices so low that poor people do not get service. Then we will look at how the rural poor lose their land and water to corrupt grabs. The solution to this problem — stronger property rights —

offers a useful bridge to our third discussion. Property rights for the poor can generate sufficient income to help them "pull" water to themselves.

After all, everyone knows that water flows towards money.

The poor will pay for good service

People in richer countries pay very little for water that gives them great benefits, but price increases tend to blind them to their good fortune. They protest instead of welcoming the opportunity to maintain reliable service, forgetting that a utility needs revenue to invest in maintenance and capital improvements. They also forget to put this price into perspective. A few years ago, I looked at water prices for 308 cities in 102 countries and found that water is "affordable" in all middle- and upper-income countries and many developing countries. Good water service need not be expensive.

The poor in corrupt developing countries would agree. They typically lack water service and do not benefit from subsidized prices or income supports because the same factors preventing service — corruption and incompetence — also impede delivery of those benefits. The poor are often left with hoping for unreliable, dangerous service or negotiating with informal water sellers that are expensive, dirty, dishonest — or all three.

The poor are often willing and able to pay the full cost of reliable, safe water, but they are often prohibited from spending their money. "You cannot pay for a right," they are told. "We will give you service for free." It is a nice thought, but water service (a private good) costs money. If the poor don't pay, then someone else must. The rich could pay but that doesn't happen in corrupt countries. It is, in fact, more likely that the rich will get cheap water. They live in areas with infrastructure and have government friends who will ensure that their human rights arrive in those pipes.

Subsidies from government or other consumers do not guarantee service for the poor. System expansion is expensive. Honest managers do not want to extend their network to neighborhoods where people are too poor to pay. At best,

they break even when charities pay. At worst, they risk the financial and operational integrity of their system. Crooked managers will ignore slums because they can't be bothered or benefit from misery. Millions of people in India and Pakistan, for example, pay 10–20 times the "social tariff" because they can only get water from tanker trucks. Some of those trucks are owned by the water managers who keep forgetting to extend service to slums.

The easiest way to get water to the poor is to let them buy fully priced water from an efficient operator, as they do in Phnom Penh. The poor can also be helped by transparency and competition. It is easier to see the difference between corrupt and honest mangers when a water monopoly is "corporatized" to have independent finances and operations. Competition from private vendors selling water from kiosks or neighborhood networks can help the poor and spur the incumbent to perform.

Weak property rights hurt the poor

The debate over rights in the countryside differs from its urban cousin. Rural people do not need to wait for a pipe to bring water to their homes. They can self-supply their own water from rivers, wells or small cooperatives, but these supplies are threatened by water scarcity. Increasing demands from farms, factories and cities are draining wells, diverting rivers, and closing fisheries. These problems can be solved by a combination of minimal environmental flows and protection of private or community water rights, but those solutions are hard to implement in a corrupt country. The basic rights that may exist are often stolen by corrupt politicians who sell "grabbed" rights to foreign investors who use land and water to grow food for export. Corrupt politicians discard subsistence farmers when they can make money from bribes.

Grabs are not new. In Roman times, barbarian land was declared *terra nullius* (empty land), and citizens were allowed to take land from people too uncivilized to have rights. Today's land grabs are driven by the same forces: weak rights and attractive profits. Higher crop prices have raised the value of grabbed water and land. Technology has made it cheaper to pump water and transport food over longer distances. Global political unrest increases the importance of cheap food to governments that bribe their populations into submission. International investors and corrupt politicians are falling into each other's arms.

Grabs could be reduced or reversed if honest politicians took over, but that action is rare. A second option would register private or communal property rights in a public place. Corrupt politicians may protest the cost of surveys and administration necessary to establish and run a register. They may also claim that poor people prefer to live on unregistered land to save rent. Neither of these excuses holds up to scrutiny. Technology means that surveys are quite cheap. Possession seems a valid excuse for a right to land in a slum. The poor may even be eager to pay if registration ends their fear of being evicted, allows them to borrow against their property, and creates an address that can receive water service.

The costs and benefits of a water register are similar to those of a land register except that water rights need to account for flows and other factors discussed in Chapter 5. A registry of land and water rights would help the poor and the honest. Transparent public records will help people see where money goes and water flows. Registers will help the poor and the nation by reducing theft and the uncertainty that inhibits productivity and development.

This advice, by the way, also applies in many rich countries where water scarcity is a new problem. We need to know who gets water (how much, where and when) if we want to put it to beneficial use.

From human rights to property rights

I have boldly claimed that the poor are willing and able to pay for good water service, but what if they are too poor? Yes, we know that they can be given money, but such entitlements are often mistargeted. They also upset taxpayers who do not care about "losers." It may be easier to get money to the poor if it represents a return on *their* wealth.

A water registry can be expanded to help the poor by giving every citizen a share of their nation's water wealth that would entitle the citizen to a share of royalties paid by whoever uses the water for drinking, irrigation, mining, and so on. These payments will be relatively small for some citizens, but disproportionately large for the poor.

The bare outline of this system would work as follows. Citizens do not collect or manage their share of water. National, regional or communal governments manage water on behalf of citizens. The level of government management will depend on the watershed, but that level will also determine social priorities for water uses.

Citizens will be involved in the transparency, efficiency and accountability of these operations. The debate and vote on social and private water allocations will attract attention. Some watersheds may set aside more water for the environment and sell less to users. After setting aside social water, managers would sell commodity water and distribute revenues to citizens. It will be necessary, as usual, to track diversions and return flows, especially if water leaves the watershed.

Prices and allocations will change with seasons, social priorities, and other influences on supply and demand. Arid areas, for example, will not have much water to sell, but prices will be high when demand is strong.

This system can be used in any country where water belongs to the people. The system can be used immediately where private water rights do not exist, but it can also replace existing rights and distributions. This idea is compatible with other rights in water (discussed in Chapter 5) because it addresses payments to owners more than allocation to uses, but some differences will need to be negotiated. (Should people who get rights for free be paid for those rights? Should rights be transferred over 5 or 50 years?) Water scarcity requires creative thinking and flexible solutions.

Market allocations of water will increase efficiency, as they have in Australia's Murray-Darling Basin. Prices will allocate water to important uses and facilitate complementary improvements. Dividends will help urban dwellers pay for water services. Those payments will help utilities improve reliability.

Small-scale farmers will have to buy water, but they will get a dividend for their share in water rights and the opportunity to buy water on fair terms (no small gain). Large-scale farmers and industrialists will have to spend more on water than they do now. Some of them will oppose these reforms because their business is based on subsidized water. Others will welcome the opportunity to expand production based on efficient water use.

The sale of commodity water will reveal buyers and discipline accountants. Citizens in the poorest, most corrupt countries will know how much money they should receive, and they will push to get it. It will not be easy to account for income or disbursements in countries with tens or hundreds of millions of people, but technology (biometric identification, mobile phone banking, and so on) makes that task easier every day. This is no dream: Alaska has paid oil-dividend checks to citizens for over 30 years.

Property rights can be fair and efficient

A human right to water is worthless in a corrupt country and redundant in an honest one. Programs to give water to the poor often benefit the rich as they weaken utilities. Citizens in developed countries can afford to pay the full cost of water. The poor in developing countries can often afford the full cost of water, but corruption or misplaced subsidies may prevent them from buying services. Service will improve if utilities are run as independent, transparent corporations facing competition. The utility's management can be replaced in a competitive tender for a limited-term concession. The utility can be forced to compete with entrepreneurs providing services through local networks or kiosks.

Traditional, communal and social water rights should be registered and protected. Commodity water rights should be divided among citizens in the absence of rights, the presence of unfair allocations, or an effort to reform an outdated system of rights. Annual flows associated with rights can be sold in markets to facilitate reallocation among changing priorities. Revenue from water sales (the rental of rights) should be allocated to citizens who can purchase water services or anything else they want.

CHAPTER 8

Pipes, canals and dams

In Chapter 3, we discussed how businesses should be allowed to use water as long as they pay competitive prices that reflect the full cost of water as a private good. This chapter discusses how businesses, cities, farms and other water users may gain private benefits from public spending on infrastructure.

Consider, for example, a "multi-functional" dam that stores water for drinking and irrigation, provides recreational space, and absorbs potential flood flows. In its first two roles, the dam provides private benefits to a utility selling water to its customers and farmers irrigating crops. In its recreational mode, the dam allows anyone to enjoy boating or fishing. In its last use, the dam provides a public good benefit by protecting downriver land and people from floods.

These benefits justify the existence of the dam, but it is difficult to estimate their relative shares. That quantification matters because dams are often rationalized in terms of their benefits to specific interest groups. More important, they are often funded by users who pay in proportion to their benefits.

Say that estimated benefits from this multi-functional example contribute to the total in shares of 40/20/20/20 percent. Given a $10 million dam, these numbers imply that the utility should pay $4 million towards the dam, farmers should pay $2 million, and the public treasury should pay $4 million for recreational and flood-protection benefits. So far, so good, but what if farmers use the same amount of water from the dam as utility consumers? Shouldn't they and the utility pay $3 million each?

Farmers will argue that they cannot afford to pay, cheap water helps feed people, nobody was going to use the water, and so on. Utility managers will be quiet since they care more about the dam's reliability than customers' money.

Another complication arrives when we look at recreation and flood control. What if only half the projected boaters and fishermen use the reservoir? Do flood-protection benefits rise if more houses are built in the flood plain? What if the dam can hold several years of inflow, effectively making a flood impossible? Should "the people" pay for protection they will never need when farmers and urbanites use water every year?

This dam example illustrates the chapter's two themes. The first is that private entities will work hard to direct public spending to their benefit. The second is that infrastructure alters the costs and benefits of subsequent actions for a very long time. Our goal is to reduce public subsidies to private benefits and improve infrastructure decisions that will affect our choices, wallets and behavior for a very long time.

Other People's Money... and Water

I first heard "OPM" when someone was describing California's Central Valley Project (CVP) for collecting water behind huge dams in northern California and distributing that water through a vast network of canals to farmers in central and southern California. The U.S. Bureau of Reclamation started the CVP in the 1930s and expanded it over four decades. The CVP was designed to boost farm incomes, but that boost was apparently too small. Farmers have not managed to repay taxpayers.

The details of this boondoggle are illuminating. Farmers were given 50 years to repay capital costs, interest free. That little gift turned out to be huge as interest really adds up over decades: $100 in 1940 was worth roughly $900 in 1990, and farmers got to repay 1940 debts with 1990 money

— except that they didn't (see below). This massive subsidy was no accident. It fit into a long-standing policy of subsidizing farmers. That policy explains why farmers were credited for revenues from CVP hydropower sales when they had "trouble" covering CVP operating costs. It explains how they were forgiven repayment altogether when costs were still "unaffordable."

Those headline subsidies came with colorful and painful details. The CVP increased water consumption by bringing water to formerly dry places at subsidized prices. Those deliveries had terrible environmental impacts because CVP engineers did not integrate ecosystems impacts into their designs. The last laugh came from Congress, which gave farmers another 50 years to repay capital costs, but it looks like they will miss the 2030 deadline. The Other People who paid for this project in the 1930s never saw their money again. Their great-grandchildren have only seen 20 cents on the (depreciated) dollar returned. Farmers, meanwhile, have profited from cheap water for 75 years and counting. Not all those profits go to selfish ends. Many farmers "give back" to their political friends.

But wait! What about California's position as the largest agricultural producer in the U.S.? What about the massive contribution of agriculture to California's economy? What about the almonds, wine and cheese that California exports? Let's put those facts into perspective. First, California farms are built atop ecosystems that had benefitted more citizens. Second, agriculture uses 80 percent of the State's water to produce 3 percent of its economic output with 5 percent of its workers. Finally, remember that subsidies benefit farmers with connections more than farmers with skill.

My point is that OPM and cheap water do not make California as great as much as increase profits to political insiders. Even worse, subsidies prevent good community farmers from replacing bad corporate farmers. That result means wasted water, expensive food, abused labor and dying communities. Is it possible to reverse those trends and redirect California onto an economically, environmentally and socially sustainable path? Yes, but such a change in direction will be difficult. Reformers don't just have to overcome the political and financial might of privileged farmers. They must also reform bureaucracies and reshape infrastructure that has been cemented in place for nearly a century. These barriers mean the CVP is likely to influence California's water flows far into the 21st century.

Is this example or analysis limited to California or the United States? Sadly, no. I have studied similar OPM-disasters all over the world, from India to China to Australia, Egypt and Peru. They are common everywhere because politicians say they are for the common good — economic development, community empowerment, and so on — when they are really just spending OPM on friends, relatives and supporters. Americans have no monopoly on corruption.

Many cities benefit from an urban version of OPM. Some use canal networks that are subsidized by other people. Others pay the full cost of infrastructure but nothing for the water taken from elsewhere — what you might call Other People's Water. These water transfers are based on property rights, historic claims or political compromise that rarely consider the costs to everyone in the exporting area or benefits to everyone in the receiving area. That is because they tend to get approved in a political forum where representatives decide on behalf of everyone else.

Such a process may seem normal except that these uses of water and infrastructure do not really have a public or social (non-excludable) component. They are private or club goods that benefit distinct groups at the expense of public water and money. These water and infrastructure gifts privatize gains and socialize losses in the same way as bailouts saved millionaire bankers and screwed taxpayers during the global financial crisis.

From OPM to pay your way

Water flows to cities — like flows to farmers — come with an "opportunity cost" that depends on the opportunity to use the water elsewhere. Urban over-consumption leaves less water for tomorrow. Irrigation water may produce more value on another field. Opportunity costs get bigger when water leaves its natural catchment or moves between sectors (from agricultural to urban use, for example) because of accounting-value mismatches. Reallocation always produces surprising benefits and costs. These surprises are much bigger with one group gets benefits and another gets costs.

Policies that draw on other people's money and water are neither fair nor efficient, but they are common. A rebalancing and matching of costs and benefits can reduce the harm of past policies. An evaluation and assignment of proportional responsibility can improve the performance of new policies. Policy reform and design should therefore move through the following stages.

First, consider the rights, preferences and expectations of people in water-sending and receiving areas. A broad political consultation is more legitimate. Second, allocate costs in proportion to private and social benefits, with a mechanism for changing cost allocations when benefits change. Third, require participation of banks or private investors in financing infrastructure. Outsiders will expect decent returns — as they do in the multi-trillion dollar municipal bond market — but their fees are worth it. Outsiders with money at risk will monitor project costs and performance. Market traders will reinforce performance monitoring by selling on danger and buying on exaggeration. Traders with an incentive to collect good information will help the public understand how well their money is being spent. Fourth, projects that fail to deliver public benefits or repay loans should be repossessed, shut down or sold. Fiscal discipline will help beneficiaries focus on meeting their promises instead of asking for bailouts. Finally, manage water projects, benefits and costs within watersheds or river basins. It makes as much sense for people in Alabama to pay for dams in Oregon as it does for people in London to pay for a canal in Beijing.

These principles would reduce national involvement in water management. Some infrastructure patriots will protest, since national money, expertise and technology have developed infrastructure in the past. They would be right, except for infrastructure projects that benefit locals over citizens.

National funding is meant to bring prosperity and scale, but it may not deliver either. California is dammed and criss-crossed by canals and aqueducts, but the state is constantly experiencing water crises. Huge projects in China, India, Pakistan, Egypt, Libya, Spain and many other countries deliver poor value for money and devastation for ecosystems. National governments should not build national projects. Instead, they can set quality standards, protect environmental flows, and delegate infrastructure management to regional bodies responsible for balancing costs and benefits in the public interest, within each watershed.

Path dependency

Infrastructure tends to bend history by permanently changing costs and benefits. Rome's Porta Maggiore is a case-in-point. The gate was built nearly two thousand years ago at the junction of two aqueducts. Today that junction is still a major hub for roads, trams and utilities. It is easier to walk a beaten path than break a new trail.

"Path dependency" describes how early decisions change the costs and benefits of future decisions and why it is difficult to change outdated policies: people pay more attention to the short-term cost of getting out of a rut than the long-run benefit of following a new path. On a small scale, consider how difficult it is to move your sink to another location in the kitchen. Now consider how easy it is to build more houses next to an existing water network — or how hard it is to move a city like New Orleans out of harm's way.

Path dependency explains how water infrastructure can have a major and lasting impact. Infrastructure changes costs and benefits, but change does not prohibit action — especially if you focus on the long term. The Dutch, for example, implemented a 100-year, €100-billion plan to protect the Netherlands from climate change after seeing Katrina's impact on the U.S. The Americans, sadly, have not done much more than spend billions on rebuilding areas

that were flooded "by accident." That short-sighted policy was recently reinforced by a Congressional action to prevent flood insurance prices from reflecting risk. Vulnerable homeowners may rejoice to have their lifestyle subsidized by others — until they are washed away.

A complete accounting would weigh the future cost of business as usual against the short-term cost of relocating a community, removing a dam, and so on. It would also include past risks that were ignored and future risks that will increase. We built cities in floodplains with the assumption that walls and levees could defend them. We built reservoirs with the assumption that precipitation would fill them. Some of these assumptions were wrong, and we lost lives, property and money. Climate change will increase the rate of assumption failure and the suffering of people depending on infrastructure that is too weak to resist nature's might. Since 2012, "Superstorm" Sandy has hit America's east coast, floods have submerged Brisbane, Calgary and central Europe, and Typhoon Haiyan has devastated the Philippines. These events will become more common and their damage more painful. We need to reduce our exposure to risk.

Nature is stronger than us. Really.

Homo sapiens is a resourceful and powerful species that dominates the world's ecosystems, but we can get a little cocky. Post-disaster leaders vow to overcome nature and show who's boss, but this is not a wise position against an adversary that doesn't know you exist. We need to save ourselves, and salvation depends on changing our attitude towards weather that is increasingly strange and dangerous. We need to prepare our identities, institutions and infrastructure for climate change.

Some people advocate a "grey" strategy of fortress resistance in which cities are protected by barriers and supplied by complex machines like nuclear-powered desalination plants. Others advocate a "green" strategy of using natural infrastructure to defend and support human settlements at a lower cost.

Examples of green infrastructure range from parking lots with porous surfaces that increase groundwater recharge and reduce sewer-system overflows to wetlands that buffer and protect coastal communities from storm-surges and hurricanes. The green path uses "natural energy" to move earth and water to places that can dampen the impacts of droughts, floods, surges and so on. The Dutch, for example, rebuild their beaches by piling sand in one spot and letting waves redistribute it.

Green infrastructure provides the same benefits as grey infrastructure with greater efficiency, which is useful when climate change will force us to do more with less. Efficiency also helps communities that need to pay for their own protection. A grey fortress needs a lot of investment before it can deliver security. That security will disappear when a change in natural flows turns a huge mass of concrete into a white elephant.

The U.S. Army Corps of Engineers spent billions of dollars "defending" cities in Florida from floods, only to find that its channels, reservoirs and levees allowed people to put themselves at risk. The Corps has been struggling (and spending) mightily to reverse damages and reduce risks, but it is hard to find someone who is optimistic about the future of Florida. The south of the state is likely to be the first part of the U.S. abandoned to rising sea levels, fierce storms and endless flooding.

Paths are nice for nostalgia, but we need to change with the landscape. Climate change is dangerous because it brings new events and new extremes into our lives. In 2014, California is experiencing its most severe drought in 500 years. England's winter is the wettest since records began in 1910. New weather records have been set in Argentina, Austria, Australia and other non-A countries. These events may reflect climate change or bad luck, but their origin matters less than their cliché-busting impacts.

We are punch drunk, six feet under a perfect storm of black swans exploiting chinks in our armor to attack our soft underbelly. We need to man up, turn the page, reset relations with the Dog Days of Summer, and run a new paradigm up the flag pole.

We need to adapt — if only to avoid terrible clichés!

Path independent and socially useful

We need to manage our infrastructure *as if* it will fail by increasing our use of adaptive techniques and technologies. Markets can allocate scarce reservoir water or determine which lands should be flooded. Risk-adjusted insurance prices can keep people from living in flood plains just as insurance payments can cover flood damages. Higher water prices can finance safety enhancements and reduce consumption depleting underground water storage. Wastewater plants can be upgraded to clean water for emergency supplies. New infrastructure can be designed and located to make it easier for people to move to safer places. All of these facilities and their policies should be run by administrators with the financial and operational independence necessary to make plans that outlast electoral cycles but an obligation to smooth water's ebb and flow into a less threatening pattern.

Users may worry that they cannot cover the high costs of infrastructure out of current cash flows. That is a legitimate worry, and the thriving government debt market demonstrates how others have solved that question. Interest costs will be low for good projects secured by thrifty municipalities and high for projects that waste public money.

The cost of adaption, like the cost of green infrastructure and institutional change, will be new and strange, but it will be a fantastic bargain. An expensive, safe life is better than a cheap, short one.

CHAPTER 9

Water wars

In our discussion of how to reduce water pollution using regulations, pricing or technology (Chapter 4), we assumed a functioning political system that would fine polluters and compensate victims. Most countries miss this qualification in one way or another. They suffer from dysfunctional institutions, political games or mere violence. Violence is the easiest to deal with — we know how to fight wars and jail criminals — but those other sources of conflict are much harder to reform or resolve because they involve powerful winners, invisible losers, and a tricky definition of rights, harm and values.

Take, for example, the famous case Los Angeles "stealing" water from Owens Valley, California. That transfer — facilitated by the Los Angeles Aqueduct and memorialized in the 1974 movie *Chinatown* — fed the growth of Los Angeles after 1913, but it was not a theft. Yes, Los Angeles buyers misrepresented their employer and promised to leave water alone that they actually exported. Yes, they overpumped groundwater, emptied a river and dried up Owens Lake. But neither their lies nor their actions were illegal. That difference did not mean much to locals who felt undercompensated for the legal destruction of their community and its environment. The 1983 decision defending Mono Lake (described in Chapter 5) may have ended the fall of Owens Valley. Subsequent decisions have brought more water to the area, but recovery is not guaranteed.

The lesson from this century-old story is that water conflict can result when laws and decisions ignore water's true role in people's lives. The same is true with international water conflicts because they share a common denominator: outdated institutions from an era of abundance that are unable to cope with water scarcity. Those institutions promise more water, of higher quality, than exists, *and* they lack a mechanism for renegotiating promises or reconciling claims. Those common roots explain why international disputes often resemble domestic failures. Chinese polluters and diverters harm fellow citizens. Chinese dams threaten neighboring countries. America's farmers pollute waters that its fishermen depend upon. America has disputes with Canada and Mexico over water rights and pollution.

Conflict over water occurs in most countries of the world. In some places, this conflict harms people, destroys property and wastes time. In others, it merely taxes life with inconveniences. Most conflict over water manifests as reasonably civilized bickering, but some of it escalates to violence. In this chapter, we will discuss various political, social and communal ways of reducing conflict and increasing cooperation.

Politicians often benefit from conflict

Corrupt politicians may direct water to friends, but the worst politicians feed conflicts to get attention and lobbying. These politicians, for example, may "listen" to farmers and environmentalists fighting over a river's water for years. Conflict delivers money, power and pleading to politicians. Resolution forces them to attend to new issues, unfamiliar dynamics, and unknown personalities.

Politics is often called a zero-sum game because politicians take from some to give to others, but the worst political interventions waste so much time, blood and money that both sides lose. These negative-sum games can be particularly wasteful with water because conflict costs often exceed the value of the water in dispute.

In their 2005 book, *Liquid Assets*, a team of Israeli, Jordanian and Palestinian scholars estimated "that the value of the water in dispute between Israelis and Palestinians is considerably less than $100 million per year." This number is tiny compared to the political cost of Israel's policy of maximizing extractions from the Jordan River and micromanagement of "Palestinian" water in the West Bank. In 2014, the U.S. will give Israel over $3 billion in military aid, including $200 million for missile defenses designed to protect Israelis from angry Palestinians.

This example is also exceptional. Conflict over water is surprisingly rare compared to conflict over oil, diamonds, or land. Israel, Jordan and Palestine cooperate on many other aspects of regional water management. Scholars agree that shared water can facilitate better diplomatic relations, but they disagree on whether water drives conflict or water conflicts reflect deeper antagonisms. We will not resolve this important question here, but it helps to think of why water is not worth fighting over. The first reason is that the value of water is too low relative to its transportation cost. The victor in a water war cannot make fast money selling it or take it home like diamonds or art. Second, water can be spoiled if one party to a dispute feels mistreated. It is much easier to pollute vast quantities of water than oil. Third, locals often share variable water flows over decades and centuries. Their social and financial relations often predate and supersede nationalist boundaries and the rhetoric of distant politicians. Locals will not join "their side" if conflict will harm them.

Defend the country, not the few

Corrupt politicians serve themselves, but what about politicians defending the nation's water from foreigners? Egyptian politicians have repeatedly threatened upstream countries that block or divert Nile waters. Threats impede peaceful trade or migration; they can also escalate into violence. They certainly make it harder to negotiate fairer or improved water management.

Many citizens want their politicians to maximize water diversions for domestic use and minimize the quality of wa-

ter flowing over the border. They may not see how their views may backfire. Say, for example, that a river flows from Mexico into the U.S. that sometimes carries less water or water of a dubious quality. It would be typical for Americans to ask the federal government in Washington, D.C., to pressure the Mexicans to improve water flows, but negotiation between capitals is unlikely to produce useful results. Officials who live far from the river have a hard time understanding local concerns and constraints. Even worse, officials may ignore or deny the problem — throwing their constituents "under the bus" in exchange for agreement on a larger deal like a free-trade agreement or arms sale.

Capitol-to-capitol negotiation takes place on the wrong scale. It would be better for Mexicans and Americans on either side of the border to meet, discuss their goals, and find a means of working together. Local solutions would not rely on treaties or threats, and they can work better for interdependent neighbors. The move of a local, hot dispute to distant, cool setting can precipitate failure. Negotiators may magnify the righteousness of their respective sides; locals may reject processes they did not influence and experience.

Adam Kehane, an expert in political disputes such as the civil war in Colombia, told me that empathy makes it easier for people to respect — even understand — other's positions. How do you build empathy? "Tell everyone in the room to pair off with the person they disagree with the most.

Then tell them to take a walk together after lunch." Small talk reveals common interests. Common interests build understanding and trust. Trust leads to solutions.

Conflict can be aggravated or stopped

Conflict can cause more damage than the value of water in dispute. Some people make a living from conflict. We need to study and address conflict on the right scale. A dispute among neighbors within a watershed should be resolved at that scale. Outside resolutions may submerge a dispute until underlying frictions resurface. The search for the right path is neither easy nor predictable, but you know you have found the right path when you would be happy to take a long walk in the other person's shoes.

CHAPTER 10

Environmental flows

We would die quickly if we took no water from the environment, just as we would die slowly if we took it all. The relevant question is "how much water should we take from the environment?" This question is not tricky because everyone has a different value for the environment — we also give different values to a cup of coffee. The question is tricky because the environment is a public good that we all enjoy, regardless of how much we have contributed to its health or deterioration. The answer to "how much should we take?" can be very different from the answer to "how much should I take and you leave?"

As an example, imagine that dozens of farmers are taking water from a river that environmentalists want to restore. The farmers, as a group, may not want to give up the private benefits they get from water flows, even if their reduced diversions create a larger gain for thousands of people. What if some farmers want to restore flows? "Go ahead," their neighbors tell them. "Just don't ask me to sacrifice." That response may mean that too little water is freed for the river. "No problem," you say after reading Chapter 5, "just pay farmers for their water." But that solution just shifts the problem from water to money. Who should pay for water that benefits everyone? "Go ahead and pay," your neighbors tell you. "Just don't ask me to pay."

Every community must balance between private and public uses (such as dividing water between crops and wetlands) at the same time as it discourages free riding (taking benefits without paying). Can free riders be forced to contribute? Yes, but there wouldn't be free riders if an enforcement mechanism existed, would there?

We have wrestled with the social dimensions of water uses throughout Part II. This chapter explores how a community of diverse values can separate environmental water flows from private economic uses. The complexity of this discussion differs from the previous chapter. Most transboundary water conflicts focus on the I-win, you-lose division of flows. Disputes over environmental flows are driven by diverging personal preferences for private and public goods. These differences will never disappear, so it is necessary to establish systems for managing environmental water flows that are transparent in reflecting the weight of citizen preferences and flexible in responding to changes in those preferences.

Humans are changing the environment

Ecosystems never reach a steady state. They are populated by species that can survive variations in water, light, temperature, and other conditions. Humans adapt, but we also use shortcuts to insulate ourselves from the environment. Air conditioning and canals help millions of people live in hot, arid deserts. Machines help us commute among heated (or cooled) homes, offices and shopping centers. We knew that these inventions cost money and energy, but we are now learning about additional, relevant costs.

The cumulative and growing impact of human activities on planetary conditions has led scientists to declare the beginning of a new era: the Anthropocene. Apart from biodiversity loss, the most important novelty in the Anthropocene is rapid climate change caused by converting fossil carbon sources into CO_2 and other greenhouse gases (GHGs). There has been a lot of talk about mitigating climate change by reducing GHG emissions, but there is no sign of significant reductions. That is why people are now talking more about adapting to the impacts of climate change, which will arrive mostly through the water cycle.

The central role of water in climate change is clear when you realize that the global water cycle is driven by temperature differentials between the warm, wet tropics and colder, drier poles. These global currents in the sky produce snow, rain, tornadoes, hurricanes, and other weather affecting our lives. Climate change increases the rate of temperature exchange because there is more heat to move than before, and stronger currents mean an intensified water cycle and unruly weather. Climate change will bring bigger storms, longer droughts, larger temperature swings, unusual seasons, and other changes that eco- and human systems have not experienced for a long time — if ever.

Humans have influenced and coped with water flows — using dams and canals — for thousands of years. The Industrial Revolution put these changes into high speed as machines and energy allowed us to use water where and when we wanted. We reduced environmental flows via extractions, diverted them via landscaping, and delayed them via infrastructure. Our individual actions may have seemed reasonable, but their cumulative impacts eventually affected natural systems previously considered immutable. Climate change is imposing a similar diktat, except that we are not in charge. It is time for humans to be humble — if we want to survive.

Rivers and wetlands benefit humans

Tens of millions of people depend on the Colorado River for their water, and the river is now "dead" from an ecological perspective. The Colorado's diverted, dammed, depleted and polluted waters don't even reach the Gulf of California. How will people cope when climate change reduces the snow that feeds that river and increases the temperatures that vaporize its water? Some people propose supply-side solutions like diverting water from "surplus" rivers to replenish the drained and maimed Colorado or using nuclear-powered desalination plants to serve cities and farms, but those actions do nothing for the ecosystem the river supports and little to check demand that is likely to exhaust new supplies.

Around the world, the Nile, Mekong, Po, Yangtze, and many more rivers are under pressure. The people who depend on them already face water scarcity. Some of these people are applying supply-side techniques to squeeze more water from the environment (cutting "thirsty" trees is a favorite), but what will they do when climate change turns up the pressure? China is doubling down on Beijing's unsustainable consumption by building a South-North Water Transfer Project that will deplete "surplus" regions and citizen's pockets. That project may end up a costly boondoggle if it is not accompanied by reductions in demand. The same caveat holds in other parts of the world. Climate change will increase water scarcity by disrupting supply (precipitation patterns) and increasing natural demand (hotter surface temperatures). Today's inhabitants of water-scarce areas will need to change their habits if they want to avoid suffering, forced migration or death.

Water scarcity means less water of a lower quality. Springs are drying, wetlands are shrinking, and groundwater "insurance" is draining away. Dying ecosystems cannot clean as much water as before, nor can they hold flood waters for later release.

In the past, the environment was so vast and our technology so puny that we could damage it without fear. "Water conservation" originally meant using water before it flowed — wasted — into oceans. Concerns about water flows and ecosystems have multiplied since them. Some people see nature as an endless resource for mining. Others worship it. Most people want to use some nature but protect the rest. They would see natural trade-offs between leaving water in a river and diverting it to cities.

It is tricky to discuss those trade-offs because it is difficult to quantify the value of environmental water flows. People who dislike seafood may not mind if pollution kills a fishery, but fishermen, their communities, and fish eaters mind. Fewer fish means fewer jobs, more expensive food, and a reduction in living standards. Are those costs acceptable to the people who pollute the water? These questions often lead to

heated debates over rights, traditions and community. They are rarely resolved by an economic calculation of costs and benefits that are hard to quantify, experienced by different groups, and subject to different risks and uncertainties.

These complications make it harder to solve problems, which is why we should be more cautious when modifying ecosystems or depleting nature. Ecosystems can recover from some variations, but big variations can cause irreversible harm. There is a big difference between a 10 percent reduction in flows that takes a river from 80 to 70 percent of normal volumes and a reduction that takes it from 10 to 0 percent. Ecosystems have evolved under fluctuating circumstances, but humans have increased the magnitude and speed of fluctuations beyond many ecosystems' capacity to adapt. Although some people may feel that a dead or altered ecosystem is a small price to pay for our material prosperity, others may disagree. We may like to play golf on lush green grass, but we can still play a challenging game on a course with big sand traps. That alternative will be more attractive if it means we can take a post-game drink next to a cool stream instead of retreating to an air-conditioned bunker surrounded by baking asphalt.

Even ignoring Garden of Eden imagery, isn't it better to protect rivers and wetlands in case we want them later? The residents of New Orleans and neighboring coastal communities probably regret that the oil and gas industry inflicted so much damage to their bayous. Those missing wetlands could not protect communities from the full force of Hurricane Katrina's rain, wind and waves.

A little more flow

We are clever at finding technologies or techniques that can extend the benefits of scarce resources. We live comfortably in a range of climates. We eat a variety of quality foods. We trade information and goods around the world. We are creative when facing constraints from costs, laws, taboos, and other sources.

Now we need to apply our skills to make changes in our lives. These changes need not be painful. I have taken showers at campgrounds where you get two minutes of hot water for each coin. I take shorter showers than I do at home because my taps are not coin activated. My camp showers use less water because I am immediately aware of the cost, the cost is high, and it is annoying to keep adding quarters.

The lesson here is not that a change of incentives affects our behavior. That is obvious. The lesson is that we can get clean with less. We cannot take as much water from the environment, so we must cope with less. Less personal water doesn't automatically harm our quality of life. People in Amsterdam use one-fourth the water of people in San Francisco, but they aren't any less happy.

Greater environmental flows will upset some people and please others. Some people will change their habits or business models. Others will gain (real or imagined) benefits from increased flows. Extraction limits can be administered with prices, regulations, or other techniques, but their level needs to be agreed upon though a political mechanism that reflects social priorities.

"Acceptable" levels should not be set by those with an interest in diverting water. They should be set by scientists who understand the connections between flows and healthy ecosystems. Scientists may be vulnerable to the bias of reserving too much water for nature. That means we should make changes if their recommendations lead to outcomes that over- or undershoot the community's ecosystem targets. These adjustments will add or subtract water available for private uses, but a two-step allocation (reserve environmental flows before allocating remaining waters among human uses) is much easier to manage than balancing between "co-equal goals." You cannot balance between irrigated crop yields and ecosystem productivity when different groups get different benefits from each.

Will this policy destroy civilization? Perhaps in editorials, lobbyist pleas, and other political debates, but not in the business world. Businessmen — farmers, water managers, and industrialists — love free water, but they can find ways to work with less. Water scarcity in Texas has led oil and gas companies to recycle their production water.

Less means more

Our past neglect has damaged the local and global environment. Now we must protect our local, water-dependent ecosystems and restore their flows. A healthy environment with functioning ecosystems delivers clean air and water, gives us food and pleasure, and protects us from variations in temperature, water flow and weather. Climate change makes these benefits even more valuable.

From afterword to forward

Thank you for spending your time with this book. Its central thesis is that we need to manage water for the private or social good it is. Private water flows for urban, industrial or agricultural users can be allocated in markets or sold at prices that reflect service costs and scarcity. The social dimensions of water show up in decisions and actions affecting human rights, infrastructure, conflict, and environmental water flows. Citizens need to help politicians, bureaucrats and managers serve social and community interests.

I discussed private uses before social uses because private uses are simpler to understand, but decisions and allocations should be made in reverse order. The first step is to establish rights, place infrastructure, divide water with neighbors, and set aside the environmental flows. Then — and only then — can we allocate remaining water among cities and farms so that people can drink, bathe, wash, produce goods, generate energy and grow food.

I wrote this book because I want to offer an economic perspective on how we can live with water scarcity. And by we, I really mean you. The examples in this book demonstrate how others succeed — and fail. I hope you can use these examples and ideas, so make a list of the water problems affecting your community. Then go learn, meet others, discuss options, and help your community manage its water. Don't wait for others to do it. You have a right and an obligation to determine *your* future.

A few words of thanks

This book arrived in waves. I started blogging about water over six years ago as a graduate student more interested in policy performance than abstract theory. As a blogger, I learned a lot about other people's opinions, knowledge and experiences. I published *The End of Abundance; Economic Solutions to Water Scarcity* in 2011 as a summary of the ideas and examples discussed at aguanomics.com.

After several years, it seemed time to revisit the issues and refresh my summary with new policy ideas. I also wanted to write a book that was more accessible in language, length, price and organization. I wanted the book to be accessible because I think my policy ideas have become more flexible (or adaptable) after several years and hundreds of discussions with people. (It turns out that many people care about water.)

I began writing this book in September 2013 while Cornelia and I were living in Vancouver, Canada. I started with a bare outline and a fresh page, as I did not want to edit the old book into a shorter version. I got some fantastic help from volunteer readers who gave me extremely useful feedback on earlier drafts, the tone of the book, and its overall message. My deepest thanks to Amanda Rice, Ben Foster, Chris Brooks, Dan Crawford, David Lloyd Owen, Janet Neuman, Jay Wetmore, Jeffrey J. Ripp, Jessica Fosbrook, Joel Fishkin, Karen Dalgaard Sanning, and Patrick Keys.

I also got some support on the title. The people on my mailing list helped me dump an old title and choose the current one. (George Csicsery, in fact, typed those exact words.) It may seem a bit trivial to remark on the title, but it captures the book's main point: we can live with water scarcity if we recognize scarcity and change the way we manager water. As someone who has to respell his last name all the time, I'll tell you that it is very nice to be able to explain my book in 20 seconds.

After the book was in draft, I sent it to people who could read the whole thing and perhaps endorse it. (Readers want to know if someone *besides* the author likes the book.) I am privileged to have the endorsements of the experts whose words are inside the front cover. I reckon they represent nearly 400-man-years of experience in the water sector, and I am pleased they like my stuff.

Speaking of man-years, I just noticed that all the recommendations are from men. That lopsided result is a bit of an accident, as I know at least 25 women active in the water sector. But it is also a little telling. Water management has been a "man's job" for a long time. Men were engineers, stronger, or more aggressive. Women's involvement in water tended to concern washing, cooking and (for poor, young girls) carrying water. Men have brought our water systems a long way — perhaps too far. Many systems are solid but rigid. The people who manage them may be experts at optimization and flow control but novices at innovation and customer service. Women tend to be empathetic listeners and compassionate leaders, which is why they are often put in charge of personnel, marketing and (increasingly) finance. It would be great if they could bring a more inclusive work ethic to a male-heavy, communications-light sector whose operations affect our lives and society in so many ways.

Right, so back to thanks. A number of these endorsers sent me their comments, ideas and feedback. Their assistance made me work for an extra month, but all their suggestions improved the book (I hope). So an additional thanks to Alberto Garrido, Chris Brooks, Damian B. Park, David Verlee, Guido Schmidt, Guillermo Donoso, Joshua Abbott, Merton D. Finkler, Michael van der Valk, Ralph Pentland, Ties Rijcken, and Tim Shah.

I don't make much money on books and make none from

my blog. In the last few years, I've rebranded myself as a "public intellectual" — a painfully pretentious title that simply means I argue on behalf of the public interest, in public. In doing so, I abandoned the path of an academic intellectual whose work tends to stay buried in obscure journals, but whose income is usually funded by governments and universities. I was lucky to get an EU-funded position at Wageningen University in the Netherlands. That salary allowed me to give my free time to blogging, policy audiences, reporters and so on. (I also got some consulting contracts and speaking engagements, which had the double virtue of paying well and exposing me to novel dimensions of water issues.) After we moved to Vancouver, I got a teaching position at Simon Fraser University, so I still strolling down this road less traveled. I am thankful that this income allows me to communicate to the public about water without having to serve drinks for rent money.

Three people helped me with art. Nico, my Scottish mate, did the cover edit and layout. My dad took my photo. (He used to shoot models professionally. Now he makes me look good.) I took the cover photo, and I'll let you decide what it signifies. Allison Choppick did the amazing illustrations. I hope you like them as much as I do.

My final thanks go to Rob Morrow and Cornelia Dinca. Rob and I have a long running "chat" on water issues, and he's also a friend. I was very pleased that he helped with comments on the last draft. Cornelia is my girlfriend. She's also very sharp, which makes me a very lucky guy. She also gave me great feedback and clarification on the last draft. Now, if I can ever talk her into starting that blog...

I dedicated my first book to my mother, who "brought me to learning, taught me to ask questions, made it safe to accept mistakes, and showed me how to fight for what I believe in." Those words are still true and increasingly valuable to me. I know many people are having a hard time in life. I am lucky to have had choices and a perspective that helps me enjoy life. My mom put me on that path.

My dad deserves a share of that credit. Fathers and sons,

I think, can have difficult relationships. It has taken some time for ours to settle in, but I have learned to separate the wisdom from the chaff in my father's words and deeds. He gave me an exotic origin, a unique last name, the gift of small talk, and a rub of charm. My dad has worked for himself all my life (and longer). This self-employed work ethic, the variety of people who inhabit it, and the way they bounce back has helped me carry on when times were tough and support weak. The best part about my father is his life philosophy, which has served him for over 80 years and a recent quadruple bypass. I hope he enjoys this book — or at least reads the last part. I am happy to blame him for many fun and interesting experiences.

He's also taught me a lot about working with new ideas, supporting people you don't agree with, and focusing on common goals. You don't sell a thousand houses without learning how to respectively disagree, search for creative options, and listen to diverse perspectives. Some people see deals as a sacrifice — claiming they are getting less money than they deserve or spending more money than they should. I have learned from my dad that it is better to focus on why the deal is good for both sides than worry about getting a bigger share. The world would be a better place if more people focused on the positive possibilities in front of them.

Index

Alberta, 49
Amsterdam, 17
Aral Sea, 54

Climate change, 103
    Anthropocene, 102
    Flooding, 90
    Weather, 93
Colorado River, 27, 54, 103
Common pool resources, 36, 48, 52, **101**
Copenhagen, 73
Corruption
    Human rights, 77
    Manager bias, 68
    Other People's Money, 86
    Water rights, 81

Davis, 27
Demand, **12**, 13
Desalination, 15, 42

Environment
    Depleted rivers, 54
    In-stream flows, 64, 104, 105
    Priority, 57, **101**, 106
    Public trust, 54

Flooding
    Climate change, 91
    Florida, 92
    Insurance, 91
    Public good, 86

Hurricane Katrina, 49, 90, 106

Imperial Valley, 58
Infrastructure
    Aswan High Dam, 37
    Bonds, 89
    Central Valley Project, 86
    Green, 92, 106
    Path dependency, 90

    Small scale, 43
    South-North Water Transfer, 104
Insurance
    Floods, 91
    Performance, 73
    Pollution, 48
Irrigation
    80 percent of total, 51
    All-in-auction, 61
    Dead zones, 47
Israel, 97

Kehane, Adam, 98

Las Vegas, 17, 24
London, 42
Los Angeles, 24, 54

Markets
    Brokers, 63
    Human rights, 83
    Infrastructure bonds, 89
    Irrigation water, 60
    Murray-Darling Basin, 63
    Versus monopoly, 72
    Wastewater, 47
Meters, 29, 44

Owens Valley, 54, 95

Perry, Chris, 58
Phnom Penh Water Supply Authority, 74
Political economy, 5, 68, 98
Pollution
    Bottled water, 33
    Cap and trade, 46
    Deepwater Horizon, 48
    Insurance, 48
    Non-point, 45
    Oil sands, 49
    Regulation, 45
    TVA tailwater, 70

Pricing
    Affordable, 79
    Conservation, 30, 38
    Increasing block rates, 24
    Matching costs to revenues, 26, **31**
    Scarcity surcharge, 27
    Versus human rights, 79
    Water budgets, 24

Regulation
    Incentives, 22, 39
    Monopoly, 16, **19**, 69
    Pollution, 45
    Red tape, 25, 39

San Diego, 14, 58
Santa Barbara, 29
Singapore, 28
Subsidies
    Average cost pricing, 14, 21
    Business, 35
    Infrastructure, 85
    Other People's Water, 88
    Outside money, 23
    Poor to rich, 79
    Wastewater, 23
Success
    Drinking water service, 29, 71, 74
    Environmental flows, 55
    Human rights, 23, 78
    Infrastructure, 90
    Pollution, 46
    Rebates, 47, 83
    Stormwater, 45
    Transboundary water, 97
    Water management, 36
    Water markets, 30, 63
    Water recycling, 42
    Water tariffs, 27
Supply, **13**
    Climate change, 103
    Economic, 2
    Monopoly, 15

Tennessee Valley Authority, 70

Utility
    Public vs. private, 18, **39**
    Regulation, 18
    Revenue instability, 19, 26
    Revenue rebate, 30
    Unbundling, 72

Water

Accounting, 57
Economic good, 9
Free, 3, 11, 27, 52
Grabs, 80
Greywater, 41
Management, 58, 70
Markets, 55, **59**
Public health, 20
Rights, **52**, 54, 56, 81
Social or economic, 5
Stormwater, 45
Water conservation
    Evaporation, 37
    Meters, 29
    Psychology, 28, 29
    Versus revenues, 26
Water quality
    Barcelona, 73
    Bottled water, 34
    Temperature, 37
Water-energy nexus, 38

Made in the USA
Middletown, DE
01 November 2014